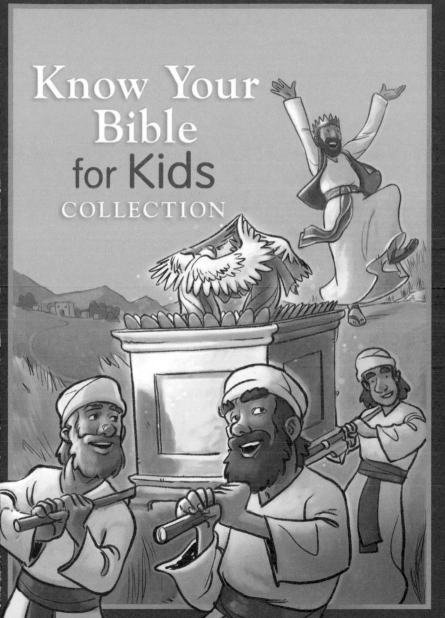

Know Your
Bible
for Kids
COLLECTION

Cover and interior illustrations: David Miles Illustration, www.davidmiles.us

Published by Barbour Books, an imprint of Barbour Publishing, Inc., P.O. Box 719, Uhrichsville, Ohio 44683, www.barbourbooks.com

Our mission is to publish and distribute inspirational products offering exceptional value and biblical encouragement to the masses.

Member of the
Evangelical Christian
Publishers Association

Printed in China.
05216 1215 IM

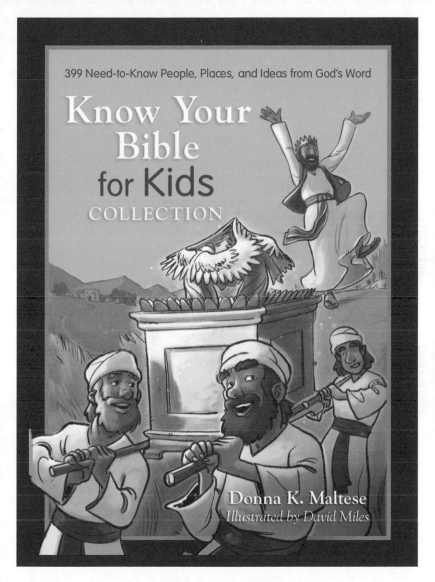

399 Need-to-Know People, Places, and Ideas from God's Word

Know Your Bible
for Kids
COLLECTION

Donna K. Maltese
Illustrated by David Miles

BARBOUR BOOKS
An Imprint of Barbour Publishing, Inc.

Contents

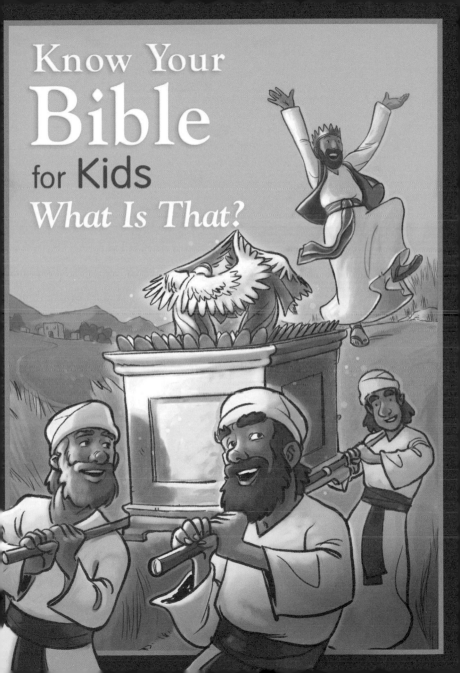

Know Your
Bible
for Kids
What Is That?

Introduction

The Bible is a wonderful book with many powerful lessons to teach us through its stories, songs, and poems. But to understand what God wants us to learn, we need to become more familiar with some of the Bible's unique words and terms.

In this fantastic resource for young readers, *Know Your Bible for Kids—What Is That?* we have chosen 101 of the most interesting and important objects, ideas, and terms found in scripture. Every fascinating "word" sketch follows this outline:

- *What is that?*
  A brief description of a specific word or term found in the Bible.

- *What is it all about?*
  Details about the background or use of that word or term.

- *What's an important verse about that?*
  A key Bible verse about that word or term.

- *What does that mean to me?*
  What that word or term teaches God's readers.

One of the great things about the Bible is the fact that God's Word—written or spoken—has the power to change people's lives. And that the more we learn about the scriptures and their message, the more God can change us and the world we live in.

The Bible's unique terms listed within these pages—from *Abba* to *Zeal*—show us how we can grow closer to God from the wisdom of His Word. Use this fun, fascinating, and fact-filled book to better understand who God is, how He wants you to serve Him, and what to expect on the adventure that awaits you—one word at a time.

Abba

What is Abba?

Abba is an Aramaic (the language Jews spoke in New Testament times) word meaning "dearest Father." It shows up only three times in the Bible.

What is it all about?

It's a word people use when they are really pouring their heart out to Father God, like Jesus did when He was in the Garden of Gethsemane.

What is an important verse about Abba?

Because we are his children, God has sent the Spirit of his Son into our hearts, prompting us to call out, "Abba, Father."
GALATIANS 4:6 NLT

What does that mean to me?

God loves you so much He sent Jesus to fill your heart, making you want to love your Abba, Father, all the more. So, call out, "Abba!"

What is the Messiah?

The person who would save Israel's people and bring them back to God.

What is it all about?

Authors of the Old Testament wrote that the Messiah would be anointed—He would have oil poured on Him as a sign of being set apart by God. He would be a prophet, a priest, and a king from King David's family. In the New Testament, many people—even demons—who met Jesus *knew* He was the Messiah!

What is an important verse about the Messiah?

These [powerful works of Jesus] are written so that you may continue to believe that Jesus is the Messiah, the Son of God, and that by believing in him you will have life by the power of his name. JOHN 20:31 NLT

What does that mean to me?

Want to be powered up? Read your Bible. It's got tons of stories proving Jesus is not only *the* Messiah but *your* Messiah! And you have life by His power!

Sin

What is sin?

Doing wrong. Sins such as lying, greed, and selfishness are just as bad as murder, lust, and stealing.

What is it all about?

A person can sin against himself, others, or God. Jesus came to earth to save people from their sins. He gives them the power to win out over their wrongdoings.

What is an important verse about sin?

I have hidden your word in my heart,
that I might not sin against you. PSALM 119:11 NLT

What does that mean to me?

Your best protection against sin is God's Word (the Bible). So find a good verse and learn it by heart. Then the next time you're tempted to do something God wouldn't like, you can say the verse. It'll give you the power to walk away!

Christian

What is a Christian?

What the New Testament people of Antioch called those who followed Jesus Christ.

What is it all about?

Barnabas and Saul were in Antioch, teaching many people about Jesus. Members of their church group were talking about Christ all the time. So people called these believers "Christians," which means the "household" of Christ.

What is an important verse about a Christian?

Suppose you suffer. Then it shouldn't be because you. . . do evil things. . . . But suppose you suffer for being a Christian. Then don't be ashamed. Instead, praise God because you are known by that name. 1 PETER 4:15–16

What does that mean to me?

Just calling yourself a Christian doesn't make you one. To be a true Christian, you must act like Jesus. That happens when you follow Him with all your heart.

Creation

What is creation?

Making something out of nothing—which is something only God can do! Humans cannot make something out of nothing. That's because everything they "make" begins with something God already created!

What is it all about?

In the very beginning, everything was dark. Then, just by God speaking words, light appeared. Next, the heavens, oceans, land, trees, plants, fish, birds, animals, and people came into being! And everything God made in six days He called good. On the seventh day, God rested from all the work He had done.

What is an important verse about creation?

God made us. He created us to belong to Christ Jesus. Now we can do good things. Long ago God prepared them for us to do. EPHESIANS 2:10

What does that mean to me?

God made you in His image, to be just like Him. So you, too, have an urge to make and do good things. What can you make to please God or to help others—or both?

Tree of Life

What is the Tree of Life?

A tree in the Garden of Eden. People who ate its fruit would have eternal life.

What is it all about?

Adam and Eve sinned by eating fruit from the Tree of the Knowledge of Good and Evil. To keep them from living forever, God sent them out of the Garden. Then He set up a flaming sword to guard the path to the Tree of Life.

What is an important verse about the Tree of Life?

"To everyone who is victorious I will give fruit from the tree of life in the paradise of God." REVELATION 2:7 NLT

What does that mean to me?

After Jesus comes back, God will let believers eat from the Tree of Life and live forever with Him in the new heaven. So stick with Jesus. With Him you can't lose!

Adoption

What is adoption?

To take in a person and raise him or her as one's own child.

What is it all about?

Believers in Jesus are adopted by God and become members of His special family.

What is an important verse about adoption?

You have not received a spirit that makes you fearful slaves. Instead, you received God's Spirit when he adopted you as his own children. Now we call him, "Abba, Father." ROMANS 8:15 NLT

What does that mean to me?

Because you have God's Spirit within you, you are His very own son or daughter, with the right to call out, "Abba, come help me!" whenever you need to. When you do, He'll come running.

Cross

What is a cross?

A long upright (vertical) piece of wood with another lying across it (horizontal), near the top. In New Testament times, criminals were put to death by nailing them on crosses.

What is it all about?

Jesus died on a cross—but He rose from the dead three days later!

What is an important verse about a cross?

Through his body on the cross, Christ put an end to the law with all its commands and rules. He wanted to create one new group of people out of the two. He wanted to make peace between them. EPHESIANS 2:15

What does that mean to me?

Jesus' death on the cross made peace between you and God (vertical) *and* between you and other people (horizontal)! That's a major praise!

Hell

What is hell?

A place where evil souls will go for punishment.

What is it all about?

Hell is where God isn't. It's described as a place where it's really hot and fiery, yet very dark. It's also where the devil and his demons will be.

What is an important verse about hell?

"Do not be afraid. I am the First and the Last. I am the Living One. I was dead, but look, I am alive forever. I have power over death and hell." REVELATION 1:17–18 NLV

What does that mean to me?

If you are a believer in Jesus, you don't need to be afraid of anything—not even hell! That's because Jesus has power over it! So stay with Jesus—in the light—and all will be well.

Alpha and Omega

What is Alpha and Omega?

Alpha is the first word in the Greek alphabet and *Omega* the last. They mean "beginning and end."

What is it all about?

It means God and Jesus were here at the beginning of the world and Their kingdom will never end.

What is an important verse about Alpha and Omega?

"I am the Alpha and the Omega, the First and the Last," says the Lord God. "I am the One who is, and who was, and who will come. I am the Mighty One." REVELATION 1:8

What does that mean to me?

No matter what happens, God and Jesus will always be there for you—from beginning to end. So you have nothing to fear.

I Am

What is the I Am?

God.

What is it all about?

When Moses asked God what His name was, God said, "I Am." That was God's way of telling Moses that He, God, has been around since the beginning of time—and will always be around!

What is an important verse about the I Am?

The people said, "You aren't even fifty years old. How can you say you have seen Abraham?"

Jesus answered, "I tell you the truth, before Abraham was even born, I Am!" John 8:57–58 nlt

What does that mean to me?

As a believer, you will never be alone. Jesus, who is also the I am, has been around since the beginning—and always will be! He'll never leave you.

Angel

What is an angel?

A being from heaven that visits earth.

What is it all about?

Sometimes God uses an angel to bring someone a message from Him. Other times He sends angels to guide, guard, or fight for people. Some angels appear to humans in dreams or visions—or face-to-face! After the devil tempted Jesus in the desert, angels came and took care of Him. Gabriel and Michael are the only two angels named in the Bible. God's Word says that we are to welcome strangers—because they may be angels!

What is an important verse about angels?

"Beware that you don't look down on any of these little ones. For I tell you that in heaven their angels are always in the presence of my heavenly Father." MATTHEW 18:10 NLT

What does that mean to me?

God has His angels always watching over you, taking special care of you. How cool that they let God know right away if you need His help!

Image of God

What is the image of God?

Something made to look and be like God.

What is it all about?

Boys and girls were made in the image of God. That's why they have the desire to make things—just like He does. To want God—just like He wants them. To love—just like He loves.

What is an important verse about the image of God?

So God created human beings in his own image. In the image of God he created them; male and female he created them. GENESIS 1:27 NLT

What does that mean to me?

Because you were made in God's image, you are very dear to Him—as is every person on earth. So be like your Creator! Love and value Him, yourself, and everyone you meet!

The Trinity

What is the Trinity?

Three beings—God the Father, Jesus Christ the Son, and the Holy Spirit. Together, they make up one big, great God. They are a tri-unity.

What is it all about?

God is three beings in one. The Father is the Creator God of the Universe. Jesus is the human image of the Father we cannot see. The Holy Spirit is God on the move, changing people and guiding them.

What is an important verse about the Trinity?

"Go and make followers of all the nations. Baptize them in the name of the Father and of the Son and of the Holy Spirit." MATTHEW 28:19 NLV

What does that mean to me?

You have three beings working together and in each other to help you. With Them on your team, there is no way you will ever get lost or be left behind! This is news you can't help but share with others—no matter where they live or who they are!

Anointing

What is anointing?

When oil is poured on someone or something for a special reason or use.

What is it all about?

Samuel anointed Saul and David to show people that God had chosen these men to be kings of Israel. Priests and altars were anointed to show they were holy or set apart for God. Anointing is also used for healing.

What is an important verse about anointing?

You honor me by anointing my head with oil. My cup overflows with blessings. PSALM 23:5 NLT

What does that mean to me?

God loves you and has anointed you. He has set you apart as someone special for all days and in all ways.

Judgment

What is judgment?

God's reaction to how people act by either rewarding or punishing them.

What is it all about?

God is a fair judge for all people.

What is an important verse about judgment?

"You have heard that our ancestors were told, 'You must not murder. If you commit murder, you are subject to judgment.' But I say, if you are even angry with someone, you are subject to judgment!" MATTHEW 5:21–22 NLT

What does that mean to me?

In God's eyes, being angry at someone is as bad as murdering that person. Want to do what pleases God? Be at peace with all people. That's a rewarding thing to do in heaven *and* on earth!

Ark of the Covenant

What is the ark of the covenant?

The wooden chest Moses built. Inside were three things: the *covenant* (the stone tablets on which the Ten Commandments were written); a pot of manna; and Aaron's rod that had budded.

What is it all about?

The ark was a symbol of God's presence among His people. Its lid was called the Mercy Seat, where priests used to sprinkle the blood of animals. Solomon built a temple and put the ark in the most holy room, behind curtains. Only the High Priest could go into the most holy room—and then only one time a year. The ark of the covenant disappeared when Jerusalem was destroyed, about 2,500 years ago.

What is an important verse about the ark?

We are not afraid to enter the Most Holy Room. We enter boldly because of the blood of Jesus. HEBREWS 10:19

What does that mean to me?

When Christ spilled His blood for you, He fixed it so that the ark, the curtain, and the most holy room are no longer needed. Now nothing stands between you and God.

Eternal Life

What is eternal life?

Living forever and ever.

What is it all about?

When people die, their bodies, in time, will crumble away. But the spirits of those who trust in Jesus will live forever. That's His promise.

What is an important verse about eternal life?

"He who puts his trust in the Son has life that lasts forever. He who does not put his trust in the Son will not have life, but the anger of God is on him." JOHN 3:36 NLV

What does that mean to me?

If you are a believer, you don't need to worry about death. Jesus has already been there and done that. Your forever life began the minute you started believing in the Lord. How cool is that?

Fruit of the Spirit

What is the fruit of the Spirit?

The fruitful (rewarding) ways people act or behave when the Holy Spirit is running their lives.

What is it all about?

God doesn't want people just obeying Him. He wants His children to bear godly fruit, just like Jesus. So He gave them the Holy Spirit. When people let the Holy Spirit guide them and flow through them, they begin being just like Jesus—full of love, goodness, kindness, and more!

What is an important verse about the fruit of the Spirit?

The fruit that comes from having the Holy Spirit in our lives is: love, joy, peace, not giving up, being kind, being good, having faith, being gentle, and being the boss over our own desires. GALATIANS 5:22–23 NLV

What does that mean to me?

When you let the Holy Spirit live through you, you'll be doing everything God's way—so you won't worry all the time about rules. Sounds fruity—but it's true!

Empty Tomb

What is the empty tomb?

After Jesus died, His body was put in a tomb, a grave cut out of rock. Three days later, when women came to visit, it was empty.

What is it all about?

A stone was rolled against the tomb but Jesus got out anyway! No one and *nothing*—not even death—can keep Jesus down!

What is an important verse about the empty tomb?

"Why do you look for the living among the dead? Jesus is not here! He has risen!" LUKE 24:5–6

What does that mean to me?

Jesus is alive—He's in you, helping you live your life the right way— God's way. With Jesus in your life, nothing can keep you down!

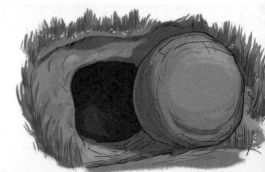

Love

What is love?

It's not just affection for another person. Love is God!

What is it all about?

The whole Bible is God's love story to humankind. It shows how much God adores His people. *And* how much He wants them to love Him, themselves, and each other.

What is an important verse about love?

No power in the sky above or in the earth below—indeed, nothing in all creation will ever be able to separate us from the love of God that is revealed in Christ Jesus our Lord. ROMANS 8:39 NLT

What does that mean to me?

No matter where you've been or what you've done, nothing, no power on heaven or earth, can keep you away from the love of God. That's how big and great and wonderful He is!

Resurrection

What is resurrection?

When people—like Jesus—are raised from the dead.

What is it all about?

Jesus died on the cross. Three days later, Jesus was resurrected—raised from the dead! He appeared alive to many people.

What is an important verse about resurrection?

Jesus said to her, "I am the resurrection and the life. Anyone who believes in me will live, even if he dies. And those who live and believe in me will never die." JOHN 11:25–26

What does that mean to me?

Jesus opened up the road for you! Dying is no longer a dead end but a doorway to God. So you need not be afraid of anything! Jesus cleared your way to Him—forever and ever!

Soul

What is the soul?

It can mean a living person or it can mean the inner self or personality.

What is it all about?

Someday a person's body will break down. But her spirit and soul will live forever!

What is an important verse about the soul?

The word of God is alive and powerful. It is sharper than the sharpest two-edged sword, cutting between soul and spirit, between joint and marrow. It exposes our innermost thoughts and desires. HEBREWS 4:12 NLT

What does that mean to me?

God's Word can help you to be really honest with yourself and God. It shows what you really think and want. Spend lots of time reading the Bible and learning about yourself and God. Doing so will help you grow your soul!

Baptism

What is baptism?

When new followers of Christ are sprinkled with or dipped in water.

What is it all about?

Being baptized in or by water shows that people are cleansed from their old life and beginning a new one—with God in Christ.

What is an important verse about baptism?

All of you who were baptized into Christ have put on Christ as if he were your clothes. GALATIANS 3:27

What does that mean to me?

When you become a follower of Christ and are baptized, you are from then on going to be more like Jesus Christ. You will be full of love, kindness, gentleness, helpfulness, and all those things that make Him—and will make you—awesome!

Believer

What is a believer?

Someone who has faith in Jesus and follows Him.

What is it all about?

A believer is not just to *say* he has faith in Jesus but to also *act* like He does.

What is an important verse about a believer?

There was a believer in Joppa named Tabitha (which in Greek is Dorcas). She was always doing kind things for others and helping the poor. ACTS 9:36 NLT

What does that mean to me?

When you follow in Jesus' footsteps—doing things He did, like helping and loving other people—you are showing people that you are a *true* believer in Christ. So who can you help today? Who can you love today?

Darkness

What is darkness?

A place where there is no light. It can also mean a place where God (or Jesus) is not present or is not known.

What is it all about?

Jesus said He was the light and that those who don't believe in Him will stay in the darkness (see John 12:46).

What is an important verse about darkness?

Those who love their brothers and sisters are living in the light. . . . But those who hate a brother or sister are in the darkness. 1 JOHN 2:10–11

What does that mean to me?

As a follower of Jesus, you are to live in the light. That means loving everyone—no matter what!

Armor of God

What is the armor of God?

The spiritual clothing God's people are to wear. It's made up of the belt of truth, the breastplate (the armor that protects your chest) of godliness, the shoes of peace, the shield of faith, the helmet of salvation, and the sword of the Spirit, which is God's Word.

What is it all about?

These are all the things God's children can wear to protect themselves from the devil's evil plans.

What is an important verse about the armor of God?

So put on all of God's armor. Evil days will come. But you will be able to stand up to anything. And after you have done everything you can, you will still be standing. EPHESIANS 6:13

What does that mean to me?

When you wear all of God's spiritual armor, you will be well protected and strong in His mighty power. With God as your defense, nothing can hurt you. So stand up straight and strong!

Heart

What is the heart?

Each person has two hearts, really. The first is the one that beats inside a person, that pumps his blood and may tremble when he's scared. The second is his emotional heart—the one where his deep-down, secret thoughts, feelings, desires, and dreams are.

What is it all about?

God wants to turn each person's entire heart—physical and emotional—from stone to flesh. To be warm, not cold. To be loving, not hateful. To be alive, not dead.

What is an important verse about the heart?

Find your delight in the LORD. Then he will give you everything your heart really wants. PSALM 37:4

What does that mean to me?

When you find your delight in the Lord, you have joy no matter what is happening in your life. It is then that God helps to make your secret, heartfelt dreams come true!

Mercy

What is mercy?

Not being punished as much as a person should, even though that person has been found guilty of something.

What is it all about?

Because of His great love for His people, God won't punish them as much as they should be punished for all they have done in the past and for what they may do in the future.

What is an important verse about mercy?

The LORD is compassionate and merciful, slow to get angry and filled with unfailing love. He does not punish us for all our sins; he does not deal harshly with us, as we deserve. PSALM 103:8, 10 NLT

What does that mean to me?

What a wonderful God you have! Thank and praise God for His mercy and all He has done for you.

Sacrifice

What is a sacrifice?

To give up one thing in order to get something better.

What is it all about?

In the Old Testament, God's children (the Israelites) sacrificed animals when they worshipped God. The animal's blood was shed (let out) in exchange for God's forgiveness of sins. When Jesus came, His death on the cross was the last sacrifice needed for forgiveness of *everyone's* sins.

What is an important verse about a sacrifice?

I am asking you to offer up your bodies to him while you are still alive. Your bodies are a holy sacrifice that is pleasing to God. When you offer your bodies to God, you are worshiping him. ROMANS 12:1

What does that mean to me?

God wants all of you—who you are, what you think, and what you do—to be used to serve Him. That's part of your worship. So go, offer yourself to God today. You'll be so glad you did!

Vine and the Branches

What are the Vine and the Branches?

The Vine is Jesus. His believers are the Branches.

What is it all about?

God wants His believers to produce fruit—to be like Him and do good things. Just like a real branch gets its food and energy from the vine, Jesus' followers get their food and energy from Him.

What is an important verse about the Vine and the Branches?

"Yes, I am the vine; you are the branches. Those who remain in me, and I in them, will produce much fruit. For apart from me you can do nothing." JOHN 15:5 NLT

What does that mean to me?

It is fruitless to make a move without Jesus. So go to Him today in prayer and get powered up! Then head out, knowing He will help you bear good fruit!

Bible

What is the Bible?

The scriptures or holy word of God.

What is it all about?

It's the story of God and His people. Different people wrote different books of the Bible—but all 66 books were inspired by God.

The Bible has two main parts: the Old Testament (before Jesus came to earth) and the New Testament (when Jesus came to earth). Written thousands of years ago, the Bible has lots of good stories and wisdom. Its overall message is that God loves His people.

What is an important verse about the Bible?

All Scripture is inspired by God and is useful to teach us what is true and to make us realize what is wrong in our lives. It corrects us when we are wrong and teaches us to do what is right. 2 TIMOTHY 3:16 NLT

What does that mean to me?

Read your Bible. When you do, it will help you find your way. And before you know it, you will find yourself growing into the person God knows you can be.

Covenant

What is a covenant?

A promise or agreement between human beings or between God and human beings.

What is it all about?

The Bible has several covenants between God and His people. In the covenant with Abraham, God promised to bless Abraham's children if he would believe in and be faithful to God. Another covenant was between God and the people of Israel. If God's people would follow God's rules (the Ten Commandments and other laws), God would forgive their sins and accept them as His people. Jesus Christ brought people a new covenant. God's law is now written on the hearts of believers.

What is an important verse about a covenant?

Christ is the go-between of a new covenant. Now those God calls to himself will receive the eternal gift he promised. They will receive it now that Christ has died to save them. . .from the sins they committed under the first covenant. HEBREWS 9:15

What does that mean to me?

If you believe in Jesus Christ, you are pure, and free to strike up a relationship with God!

Heaven

What is heaven?

Heaven is the sky above, where there are clouds, thunder, lightning, and flying birds. Even farther up there are stars and planets. And Jesus said heaven is where God lives and the place Jesus came from.

What is it all about?

God is in heaven and someday believers will join Him there. Later they will all be getting together in God's new heaven and earth!

What is an important verse about heaven?

"Don't store up treasures here on earth.... Store your treasures in heaven, where moths and rust cannot destroy, and thieves do not break in and steal. Wherever your treasure is, there the desires of your heart will also be." MATTHEW 6:19–21 NLT

What does that mean to me?

Jesus doesn't want you to collect and stack up phones, games, computers, DVDs, and books. He wants you to store up heavenly treasures—like loving and helping others, obeying God, donating clothes to the poor. What treasure can you store up in heaven today?

Trust

What is trust?

Feeling as if you can really count on or believe in someone or something.

What is it all about?

God wants His children to totally trust Him for everything—food, clothing, shelter, love, and more!

What is an important verse about trust?

May the God who gives hope fill you with great joy. May you have perfect peace as you trust in him. May the power of the Holy Spirit fill you with hope. ROMANS 15:13

What does that mean to me?

When you put all your trust in God, you won't be let down but lifted up—to a life of perfect peace. So don't worry. Just trust God. When trusting Him, the only way is up!

Blessing

What is a blessing?

A really good thing given to someone by a loving God or person. It can also be a prayer someone speaks over people, food, drink, houses—or anything else.

What is it all about?

God gives His people lots of blessings—food, a house, water, pets, moms, dads, and Jesus.

What is an important verse about a blessing?

Don't repay evil for evil. Don't retaliate with insults when people insult you. Instead, pay them back with a blessing. That is what God has called you to do, and he will bless you for it. 1 PETER 3:9 NLT

What does that mean to me?

When you bless all people—good or bad—God will bless you! Look for someone to bless today.

Blood

What is blood?

The liquid that flows through the body of a living person or animal.

What is it all about?

To God, everyone's life is precious and their blood should never be spilled. Back in Old Testament times, the blood of killed animals was used to seek God's forgiveness, free people from their sins, and make them right with God.

What is an important verse about blood?

At one time you were far away from God. But now you belong to Christ Jesus. He spilled his blood for you. That has brought you near to God. EPHESIANS 2:13

What does that mean to me?

Jesus died for you—to save you from your sins! Thank Jesus for giving His life to make things right for you!

Temptation

What is temptation?

A person's wanting to give in to something he knows he shouldn't do.

What is it all about?

The devil has been tempting people since the beginning—when the serpent tempted Eve to eat the apple in the Garden of Eden. When the devil tempted Jesus in the desert, Jesus spoke Bible verses to keep the demon in his place.

What is an important verse about temptation?

God is faithful. He will not allow you to be tempted more than you can take. But when you are tempted, He will make a way for you to keep from falling into sin. 1 CORINTHIANS 10:13 NLV

What does that mean to me?

Don't give in to temptation. Instead, look around for the nearest exit. God will always give you a way out!

Disciples

What are disciples?

People who follow and give themselves over to the teachings (or discipline) of a certain leader or way of life.

What is it all about?

During Jesus' time on earth, He called 12 disciples whose names were Simon (Peter), Andrew (Peter's brother), James (son of Zebedee), John (brother of James and son of Zebedee), Philip, Bartholomew, Thomas, Matthew (the tax collector), James (son of Alphaeus), Thaddaeus, Simon (the zealot), and Judas Iscariot (who ended up betraying Jesus). Later Jesus picked out 72 other disciples and had them spread His message.

What is an important verse about disciples?

When the seventy-two disciples returned, they joyfully reported to him, "Lord, even the demons obey us when we use your name!" LUKE 10:17 NLT

What does that mean to me?

God is awesome in power. He can use anyone, anywhere, to do amazing things in the name of His Son Jesus. How can God use you today?

Good News

What is the Good News?

The fact that God's kingdom has come!

What is it all about?

The Good News meant that the Jews' Messiah, Jesus Christ, had come, that believers could be free from sin, that God's Holy Spirit now lives in their hearts, and that someday Jesus will rule a perfect kingdom!

What is an important verse about the Good News?

"Go into all the world and preach the Good News to everyone. Anyone who believes and is baptized will be saved." MARK 15:15–16 NLT

What does that mean to me?

Believers are to tell everyone the Good News. Who can you tell the Good News to today?

Worship

To love or devote yourself to some person, place, or thing.

What is it all about?

The Bible says people were made to worship God—not money, power, fame, themselves, heroes, or idols. People can worship God by going to church, saying prayers, singing songs, clapping hands, and more!

What is an important verse about worship?

The Wise Men went to the house. There they saw the child with his mother Mary. They bowed down and worshiped him. Then they opened their treasures. They gave him gold, incense and myrrh. MATTHEW 2:11

What does that mean to me?

God wants us to worship Him each and every day. How can you show Him He is your one and only God today?

Body of Christ

What is the body of Christ?

All the people at your church and all other churches who believe in and follow Jesus Christ.

What is it all about?

Jesus, as the "head" of the body of Christ, is the one who steers all believers.

What is an important verse about the body of Christ?

If one part suffers, every part suffers with it. If one part is honored, every part shares in its joy.

You are the body of Christ. Each one of you is a part of it. 1 CORINTHIANS 12:26–27

What does that mean to me?

As a part of the body of Christ, you are linked to all other believers. When you help them, you help yourself. So, what can you do today to help people in your church—and beyond?

Glory of the Lord

What is the glory of the Lord?

The great wonder of God or His bright presence amid His people.

What is it all about?

God is an amazing being! He was the pillar of fire. He was also the cloud that led the Israelites and hung over His temple. Later, Jesus showed His own glory to His followers when He glowed like the sun.

What is an important verse about the glory of the Lord?

Jerusalem, the Holy City. . .shone with the glory of God. It gleamed like a very valuable jewel. REVELATION 21:10–11

What does that mean to me?

When you and all other believers are with God in the new heaven and earth, God's glory will light up the whole town! No electricity needed!

Christn

What is the Christ?

The title given to Jesus.
It comes from the Greek
word *Christos*, which in
Hebrew is *Messiah*.
Both words mean
"the Anointed One."

What is it all about?

By calling Jesus "the Christ," the New Testament is telling people that Jesus was God's Son and the true Savior of God's people. When Jesus was baptized, the heavens opened, God's Spirit came down like a dove, and a voice from heaven said, "This is My much-loved Son" (Matthew 3:17 NLV). That was Jesus' anointing by God. Afterward, Christ started His work as prophet, priest, and king.

What is an important verse about the Christ?

Simon Peter said, "You are the Christ, the Son of the living God." MATTHEW 16:16 NLV

What does that mean to me?

Because Jesus is the Christ, the Son of God, if you believe in Him, you will be saved. Praise Him for loving and saving you!

What is the Tower of Babel?

A tower that was being built by people to reach heaven. This happened thousands of years ago, in the days when everyone spoke the same language.

What is it all about?

The prideful Babylonians were trying to prove they could do anything—just like God.

What is an important verse about the Tower of Babel?

The LORD mixed up the language of the whole world there. That's why the city was named Babel. From there the LORD scattered them over the face of the whole earth. GENESIS 11:9

What does that mean to me?

When you get full of pride, God has a way of bringing you back down to earth. So delight the Lord. Say good-bye to pride and give God the praise.

Burning Bush

What is the burning bush?

The fiery bush out of which God spoke to Moses.

What is it all about?

When Moses was tending sheep on Mount Sinai, the angel of the Lord spoke from a fire in the middle of a bush—but the bush did not burn up.

What is an important verse about the burning bush?

"This is amazing," Moses said to himself. "Why isn't that bush burning up? I must go see it."

When the LORD saw Moses coming to take a closer look, God called to him from the middle of the bush, "Moses! Moses!" EXODUS 3:3–4 NLT

What does that mean to me?

Maybe God is doing something to catch *your* eye. Stand still. Look around. What is God trying to show or tell you?

Prayer

What is prayer?

Talking—and listening—to God.

What is it all about?

God knows what is happening in the lives of His people. But He still wants them to come to Him and tell Him how they are feeling and what they want. He also wants them to listen to what He has to say—through His Word, happenings, and other people. Jesus taught His followers how to pray to God (see the Lord's Prayer in Matthew 6:9–13).

What is an important verse about prayer?

The Holy Spirit helps us when we are weak. We don't know what we should pray for. But the Spirit himself prays for us. He prays with groans too deep for words. ROMANS 8:26

What does that mean to me?

God wants to hear from you every day—about anything and everything. But if you are ever not sure *how* or *what* to pray, don't worry. The Holy Spirit knows exactly what you're trying to say, and He'll tell God for you. And don't forget—when you're done talking, spend some time listening!

Chosen People

What are the chosen people?

People whom God picked to have a special relationship with Him.

What is it all about?

In the Old Testament, the Jews were the chosen people. In the New Testament, believers in Christ are called the chosen people.

What is an important verse about the chosen people?

You are a chosen people. You are royal priests, a holy nation, God's very own possession. As a result, you can show others the goodness of God, for he called you out of the darkness into his wonderful light. 1 PETER 2:9 NLT

What does that mean to me?

God chose you especially to be His son or daughter. What can you do to thank God? How can you show someone His goodness and spread His light?

Idol

What is an idol?

Something or someone that's man made and worshipped instead of God.

What is it all about?

God is a very jealous God. He doesn't want people worshipping and loving anything more than Him. This is so important that God made it one of His Ten Commandments.

What is an important verse about an idol?

"You must not make for yourself an idol of any kind or an image of anything in the heavens or on the earth or in the sea. You must not bow down to them or worship them." EXODUS 20:4–5 NLT

What does that mean to me?

God wants all your love for Himself. When you give Him your all, He'll give you *His* all!

Salt and Light

What is salt and light?

Salt is a mineral that makes food taste better and keeps it from rotting. Light is something warm, bright, and glowing—like sunlight.

What is it all about?

Jesus wants His followers to spread the Gospel so that others will live better and longer (eternal) lives—that's the salt part. Jesus also wants His followers to be lights in this world so that others can see God's people doing good deeds—that's the light part.

What is an important verse about salt and light?

"Let your good deeds shine out for all to see, so that everyone will praise your heavenly Father." MATTHEW 5:16 NLT

What does that mean to me?

Look around you. Where can you flavor things up by sprinkling some salt and shedding some of God's Son-light? Who can you do something nice for today?

Yahweh

What is Yahweh?

A Hebrew name for the very holy and powerful God.

What is it all about?

After the Jews' temple was destroyed in AD 70, the word *Yahweh* was never spoken out loud. In most English Bibles, the word *Lord* or *Lord* appears instead of the word *Yahweh*.

What is an important verse about Yahweh?

The name of the Lord is a strong fortress; the godly run to him and are safe. PROVERBS 18:10 NLT

What does that mean to me?

There is no one or nothing stronger or more powerful than Yahweh. So if you are ever afraid or uncertain, don't wait! Run right to Him! He will guard and protect you. With Yahweh, you are always home safe.

Rainbow

What is a rainbow?

A beautiful arc of colors that sometimes appears in the sky after rain.

What is it all about?

After the Flood, God promised He would never let it rain so hard again. The sign of His promise or His covenant is the rainbow.

What is an important verse about a rainbow?

"Never again will the water become a flood to destroy all flesh. When the rainbow is in the cloud, I will look upon it to remember the agreement that will last forever between God and every living thing of all flesh that is on the earth." GENESIS 9:15–16 NLV

What does that mean to me?

Whenever you see a rainbow, remember how God keeps His promises. *And* that *He's* seeing the same rainbow you are!

Church

What is the Church?

It's all the believers in the whole wide world. It can also be any single group of believers.

What is it all about?

A church doesn't have to have or be a building. It can be wherever believers meet. In the early days of the Church, people met in each other's houses. Wherever believers meet is their church.

What is an important verse about the Church?

Since you are so eager to have the special abilities the Spirit gives, seek those that will strengthen the whole church. 1 CORINTHIANS 14:12 NLT

What does that mean to me?

God wants you to use your spiritual gifts to serve Him and others at your church. Check out the list of gifts in the spiritual gifts entry on page 120. Which ones do you have?

Cornerstone

What is a cornerstone?

The largest, sturdiest, and most solid stone that's put on the corner of a building.

What is it all about?

Jesus Christ is the Cornerstone of the Christian faith. On Him, the body of the Church is built for all people.

What is an important verse about the Cornerstone?

Therefore, this is what the Sovereign LORD says: "Look! I am placing a foundation stone in Jerusalem, a firm and tested stone. It is a precious cornerstone that is safe to build on. Whoever believes need never be shaken." ISAIAH 28:16 NLT

What does that mean to me?

Because you believe in Jesus—the One who is so solidly the way, the life, and the truth—nothing on earth can ever shake you up.

Death

What is death?

For a body, death happens when a person's heart and brain stop working. For a spirit, death happens when it is separated from God.

What is it all about?

Someday people's physical bodies will stop working, but if they belong to Christ, their spirits will live on—forever and ever—with God!

What is an important verse about death?

We share the same kind of flesh and blood because Jesus became a man like us. He died as we must die. Through His death He destroyed the power of the devil who has the power of death. HEBREWS 2:14 NLT

What does that mean to me?

When you live for Christ, you do not need to fear death. It has *no* power over you. So be brave!

Gentile

What is a Gentile?

A person who is not Jewish.

What is it all about?

In the beginning, people fell into two groups. The first was Abraham's descendents—called the Jews or chosen people. The other group was the Gentiles—people who were not Jews or chosen. After Jesus, all people—both Jews and Gentiles—were seen as God's children.

What is an important verse about a Gentile?

God knows people's hearts, and he confirmed that he accepts Gentiles by giving them the Holy Spirit, just as he did to us. He made no distinction between us and them, for he cleansed their hearts through faith. ACTS 15:8–9 NLT

What does that mean to me?

If you have faith in Jesus Christ, you can share in the same promises and blessings that were given to Abraham. As a believer, you are one of God's chosen people!

Ten Commandments

What are the Ten Commandments?

Ten main rules that God wants His people to obey.

What is it all about?

Using His finger, God wrote the Ten Commandments
(covenant) down on two stone tablets, which He gave
to Moses. The commandments are: have only one God;
don't make idols; don't use "God" as a curse word; rest on
Sunday; honor your mom and dad; don't murder; don't
cheat on your spouse; don't steal; don't lie; and don't long
for anything your neighbor has.

What is an important verse about the Ten Commandments?

" 'Love the LORD your God with all your heart, all your soul,
and all your mind. . . . Love your neighbor as yourself.' The
entire law and all the demands of the prophets are based on
these two commandments." MATTHEW 22:37, 39–40 NLT

What does that mean to me?

If you obey Jesus' two commandments, you'll be obeying all
ten of those given to Moses. It all comes down to LOVE!
Simply LOVE!

City of David

What is the City of David?

Another name for the town of Bethlehem, which was King David's hometown and the place where Jesus was born. It is also the name of a place in Jerusalem from which King David ruled.

What is it all about?

David was Israel's greatest king. That's why the city was still called David's—even after his death.

What is an important verse about the City of David?

The Jebusites taunted David, saying, "You'll never get in here! . . ." But David captured the fortress of Zion, which is now called the City of David. 2 SAMUEL 5:6–7 NLT

What does that mean to me?

Like David, don't let anything—or anyone—stand in the way of doing what God wants you to do.

Holiness

What is holiness?

Staying away from what is worldly (unclean), and sticking close to what is godly (pure).

What is it all about?

God sent Jesus to clean up His people—so He could see them without all those sin stains. Now believers are to stick close to Jesus—the best example of holiness! People won't be totally holy until they are in heaven.

What is an important verse about holiness?

Our parents trained us for a little while. They did what they thought was best. But God trains us for our good. He wants us to share in his holiness. HEBREWS 12:10

What does that mean to me?

No matter how old you are, Father God will keep giving you life lessons so you will grow more holy, more like Jesus!

Kingdom of God

What is the Kingdom of God?

The peace of God believers feel inside when they have been reborn in the Spirit. It is also the new heaven and earth where believers will someday live with Jesus after He comes back.

What is it all about?

When people are living in the Kingdom of God, it means they are living by His power (see 1 Corinthians 4:20). They are following, being like, and believing in Jesus.

What is an important verse about the Kingdom of God?

"Seek the Kingdom of God above all else, and live righteously, and he will give you everything you need." MATTHEW 6:33 NLT

What does that mean to me?

You don't have to worry about money or anything else. Just always put Jesus first and live right (making sure you are loving God, yourself, and others). Then God will take care of everything and anything else you need in this life—and the next!

Lamb of God

What is the Lamb of God?

John the Baptist saw Jesus and knew He would be the sacrifice, *the Lamb of God*, that "takes away the sin of the world!" (John 1:29).

What is it all about?

In Old Testament times, animals were killed so God could forgive His people's sins. In the New Testament, Jesus became the last sacrifice needed to erase people's sins.

What is an important verse about the Lamb of God?

God paid a ransom to save you from the empty life you inherited from your ancestors. And the ransom he paid ...was the precious blood of Christ, the sinless, spotless Lamb of God.
1 PETER 1:18–19 NLT

What does that mean to me?

Jesus died for you! Thank Him today!

Comforter

What is the Comforter?

The Comforter is one of the names of the Holy Spirit.

What is it all about?

Some Bibles use the word *Friend* or *Helper* instead of Comforter. But they all mean the same thing. The Comforter, or Holy Spirit, is the one who helps people understand things about, of, and from God.

What is an important verse about the Comforter?

"The Helper (Holy Spirit) will tell about Me when He comes. I will send Him to you from the Father. He is the Spirit of Truth and comes from the Father." JOHN 15:26 NLV

What does that mean to me?

When you suddenly understand something about God or Jesus, that's the Comforter turning a light on in your mind, helping you to "get" God! Watch Him light up your mind today!

Forgiveness

What is forgiveness?

Overlooking a wrong someone has done.

What is it all about?

God wants every person to forgive others who have wronged her. He also wants her to forgive others she has wronged. Here's how it works: when people forgive each other, then God forgives them.

What is an important verse about forgiveness?

Peter came to Jesus and said, "Lord, how many times may my brother sin against me and I forgive him, up to seven times?" Jesus said to him, "I tell you, not seven times but seventy times seven!" MATTHEW 18:21–22 NLV

What does that mean to me?

Even if someone wrongs you 490 times, you are to still forgive him—from the bottom of your heart! Who should you forgive today?

Promised Land

What is the Promised Land?

The land that God said He'd give to Abraham and his children.

What is it all about?

God promised His people a wonderful place to rest, a really good land flowing with milk and honey. But in Moses' time, only two of the wandering Israelites made it there.

What is an important verse about the Promised Land?

" 'I took an oath and promised to give the land to Abraham, Isaac and Jacob. But not one of these men will see it except Caleb and Joshua. . . . They followed me with their whole heart.' " NUMBERS 32:11–12

What does that mean to me?

If you follow God with all your heart, mind, and soul, He'll lead you to your own promised land! So get your godly walking shoes on!

Light

What is the light?

Things that are good and cheer you up—especially God and Jesus.

What is it all about?

The prophet Isaiah wrote that "the Lord will be your light forever" (Isaiah 60:19 NLV). Jesus called Himself "the Light of the world" (John 8:12 NLV).

What is an important verse about the light?

"You are the light of the world—like a city on a hilltop that cannot be hidden." MATTHEW 5:14 NLT

What does that mean to me?

As one of Jesus' followers, you become "the light of the world" when you let Jesus shine through you. Your amazing light cannot help but shine out. So go, lighten up! Make the world glow with your love!

Devil

What is the devil?

A spirit against God.

What is it all about?

The devil wants to come between people and God. He wants to talk them into doing things that will mess up God's plans. (The devil talked Eve into eating the forbidden fruit.) The devil's other names are Satan or the Accuser, the father of lies, the Serpent, the Dragon, and the Enemy.

What is an important verse about the devil?

Give yourselves to God. Stand against the devil and he will run away from you. Come close to God and He will come close to you. JAMES 4:7–8 NLV

What does that mean to me?

To mess up the devil's plans, simply put on the armor of God, stand firm, and stay really close to God! Then watch the devil back down!

Golden Calf

What is the golden calf?

Something Aaron made while his brother Moses was talking to God on the mountain.

What is it all about?

After God rescued His people from the Egyptians, Moses met with God. But the people got scared while he was away. So they asked Aaron to make them a *new* god to love.

What is an important verse about the golden calf?

"They have melted gold and made a calf for themselves. They have worshiped it, have given gifts to it, and have said, 'This is your god, O Israel, who brought you out of the land of Egypt!'" EXODUS 32:8 NLV

What does that mean to me?

When you are scared, don't look anywhere else but to God to keep you safe. He's the only real rescuer, the only God worthy of your love!

Grace

What is grace?

The love and kindness God gives us.

What is it all about?

Grace is something God gives His people—even though they don't deserve it! There is nothing they can do to earn God's grace.

What is an important verse about grace?

God saved you by his grace when you believed. And you can't take credit for this; it is a gift from God. Salvation is not a reward for the good things we have done, so none of us can boast about it. EPHESIANS 2:8–9 NLT

What does that mean to me?

God's grace is a free gift—from Him to you! So don't worry about trying to *earn* grace. Just keep thanking God for giving you this major freebie!

High Priest

What is a high priest?

The top Hebrew priest.

What is it all about?

The first high priest was Melchizedek. He blessed Abraham. Later, Aaron was the high priest in charge of all the priests who served in the temple. He was the only one allowed to go into the Holy Room behind the curtain where God lived. After him there were more high priests. The last one was Jesus.

What is an important verse about a high priest?

That is where Jesus has gone. He went there to open the way ahead of us. He has become a high priest forever, just like Melchizedek. HEBREWS 6:20

What does that mean to me?

Jesus is now the one in the Holy Room where God dwells. So pray to Jesus—He'll take everything you say to God's ears.

Donkey

What is a donkey?

A horse-like animal that carries people or things, or pulls a plow.

What is it all about?

Donkeys were a symbol of wealth and peace. Having lots of them meant you were pretty rich. Solomon rode on a donkey when he was named king of Israel. The prophet Balaam had a talking donkey (see Numbers 22).

What is an important verse about a donkey?

"Tell the people of Jerusalem, 'Look, your King is coming to you. He is humble, riding on a donkey—riding on a donkey's colt.'" MATTHEW 21:5 NLT

What does that mean to me?

Jesus rode into Jerusalem on a donkey to show people He was their King. What can you do today to show Jesus that He is *your* king?

Hope

What is hope?

Knowing and expecting good things to happen with God's help.

What is it all about?

When believers have hope and faith in God, they can get through anything!

What is an important verse about hope?

Faith is being sure of what we hope for. It is being certain of what we do not see. That is what the people of long ago were praised for. HEBREWS 11:1–2

What does that mean to me?

Even if you're not sure where God is taking you, keep your hopes up and your faith in Him. Know that He is leading you someplace pretty awesome. Long ago, God led many people who hoped and trusted in Him. He did it for them. He will do it for you!

Joy

What is joy?

Having a good feeling or attitude about things.

What is it all about?

It's easy to be happy when everything is going well. That's because *happ*iness is based on what's *happ*ening. But God wants believers to be happy no matter what is going on—that's joy!

What is an important verse about joy?

Be full of joy always because you belong to the Lord. Again I say, be full of joy! PHILIPPIANS 4:4 NLV

What does that mean to me?

Because you believe in and belong to Jesus, you can have joy all the time! Why not start having and spreading that joy today! Doesn't that feel good?

Dove

What is a dove?

A pretty bird that looks a lot like a pigeon.

What is it all about?

In Israel, some doves were wild, some were kept as pets, some were sacrificed, and some were eaten. While in the ark, Noah kept sending a dove out to see if the floodwater had gone down. One day, when he sent the dove out and it didn't come back, Noah knew it would soon be safe to step out of the ark. Mary and Joseph took a dove to the temple for sacrifice when Jesus was born.

What is an important verse about a dove?

John agreed and baptized Jesus. When Jesus came up out of the water, the heavens opened. He saw the Spirit of God coming down and resting on Jesus like a dove. A voice was heard from heaven. It said, "This is My much-loved Son." MATTHEW 3:15–17 NLV

What does that mean to me?

When you see a dove, remember the Holy Spirit. He will be gentle with you. He brings messages. He is here to help every boy and every girl.

Zeal

What is zeal?

Showing a real passion or a real eagerness for something.

What is it all about?

God wants His followers to be very excited about serving Him, worshipping Him, and obeying His Word.

What is an important verse about zeal?

Since you are so eager to have the special abilities the Spirit gives, seek those that will strengthen the whole church. 1 CORINTHIANS 14:12 NLT

What does that mean to me?

Find something you can do to serve Christ. And then do it with all your heart, mind, soul, and spirit! That's the *zeal* thing to do!

Prophet

What is a prophet?

Someone (male or female, old or young) through whom God sends a message about what is to come (prediction).

What is it all about?

Old Testament prophets talked about a savior who was to come and what would happen to him. Then when Jesus came along, those "predictions" began coming true, which meant *He* was the Savior.

What is an important verse about a prophet?

Do not believe everyone who claims to speak by the Spirit. You must test them to see if the spirit they have comes from God. For there are many false prophets. 1 JOHN 4:1 NLT

What does that mean to me?

Watch for true prophets only—those whose predictions are right and who get their ideas from God and the Spirit.

Sermon on the Mount

What is the Sermon on the Mount?

The really awesome message Jesus gave to people on a mountainside.

What is it all about?

In this sermon (found in Matthew 5–7), Jesus tells people how to be happy and live for God.

What is an important verse about the Sermon on the Mount?

"You have heard that it has been said, 'You must love your neighbor and hate those who hate you.' But I tell you, love those who hate you." MATTHEW 5:43–44 NLV

What does that mean to me?

It's easy to love people who are nice to you. But God *really* wants you to love people who are *not* nice to you. When you do, you are being just like Jesus! And that's a good thing!

Evil

What is evil?

Any bad thing a human does that hurts himself, others, or God.

What is it all about?

Evil can also be called *sin*. God does not like evil.

What is an important verse about evil?

Don't pay back evil with evil. Be careful to do what everyone thinks is right. If possible, live in peace with everyone. Do that as much as you can. ROMANS 12:17–18

What does that mean to me?

If someone does something bad to you or your loved ones, don't do something bad to that person. You don't need to. God will take care of it. All you need to do is pay the person back by doing something nice for him or her. Try it! You will be amazed at what happens!

Passover

What is the Passover?

When the Lord passed over the homes of the Jews when they were slaves in Egypt.

What is it all about?

When Pharaoh, the ruler of Egypt, would not let Moses and his people go, the Lord struck down the firstborn in every house. The only firstborn that were safe were those in the homes of the Jews that had lamb's blood on the doorway. Those houses were "passed over." Afterward, Pharaoh let Moses' people leave Egypt—and take lots of stuff with them. Jews celebrate Passover and their freedom every year.

What is an important verse about the Passover?

It was by faith that Moses commanded the people of Israel to keep the Passover and to sprinkle blood on the doorposts so that the angel of death would not kill their firstborn sons. HEBREWS 11:28 NLT

What does that mean to me?

God will do anything to keep you, His child, safe and free! You can count on it—this year and every year!

Faith

What is faith?

Trusting in or believing in someone or something.

What is it all about?

For Christians, faith means trusting and believing in God, Jesus, and the Holy Spirit. The bigger a person's faith, the more awesome his or her life will be.

What is an important verse about faith?

"I tell you the truth, you can say to this mountain, 'May you be lifted up and thrown into the sea,' and it will happen. But you must really believe it will happen and have no doubt in your heart." MARK 11:23 NLT

What does that mean to me?

Mountains are like big problems. They can really get in your way, if you let them. But if you trust God in and for everything and don't doubt at all, He will help you lift those mountains up and throw them into the sea. In other words, He'll clear your path for you. That's how strong He is!

Holy Spirit

What is the Holy Spirit?

The invisible-to-the-eyes Spirit of God working in, on, and around people.

What is it all about?

The Holy Spirit is one of the three beings of the Trinity. (The other two are God and Jesus.) He sometimes appears as a dove, like the one that landed on Jesus when He was baptized. Other times He appeared as a flame. When Jesus left the earth, the Holy Spirit stayed behind to help God's children. That's why Jesus called Him the Helper.

What is an important verse about the Holy Spirit?

When they came up out of the water, the Holy Spirit took Philip away.... Philip found himself at the city of Azotus. ACTS 8:39–40 NLV

What does that mean to me?

When you obey God and keep your ears (and eyes) open to the Holy Spirit, He will take you wherever God wants you to be.

Mustard Seed

What is a mustard seed?

A tiny seed about the size of the period at the end of this sentence.

What is it all about?

When a mustard seed is put in the ground, it can grow into a very large plant! Jesus used it to describe the kingdom of heaven and the power of faith.

What is an important verse about a mustard seed?

"If you have faith as a mustard seed, you will say to this mountain, 'Move from here to over there,' and it would move over. You will be able to do anything." MATTHEW 17:20 NLV

What does that mean to me?

The source of your faith is God. So even if you have very little faith, God can use it to do mighty mountain-moving things!

The Flood

What is the Flood?

When water covered the land after it had rained for 40 days and 40 nights.

What is it all about?

Humans were really misbehaving—except for Noah and his family. So God told Noah to build an ark (a really big boat). Later, the ark kept Noah, his family, and all the animals inside of it safe from the rising waters. Everyone and everything else drowned.

What is an important verse about the Flood?

It was by faith that Noah built a large boat to save his family from the flood. He obeyed God, who warned him about things that had never happened before. HEBREWS 11:7 NLT

What does that mean to me?

Listen to and obey God. He will keep you safe.

Temple

What is the Temple?

The house of God that King Solomon built.

What is it all about?

God gave Solomon directions on how to build the Temple, which would take the place of the Tabernacle. Solomon's temple was destroyed about 2,500 years ago. Later it was rebuilt. The second Temple was destroyed about 2,000 years ago.

What is an important verse about the Temple?

Don't you know that you yourselves are God's temple? God's Spirit lives in you.... And you are that temple.
1 CORINTHIANS 3:16–17

What does that mean to me?

God wants you to take care of your body. That's because His Spirit is living in you! So read your Bible every day, eat right, and get plenty of sleep. God wants His awesome *temple* (you!) to last!

Compassion

What is compassion?

Feeling sad or sorry for someone or something.

What is it all about?

God had compassion for His people—even when they did things He didn't like. Jesus also felt very sorry for people. When His friend Lazarus died, "Jesus wept" (John 11:35 NLT).

What is an important verse about compassion?

Jesus saw the huge crowd as he stepped from the boat, and he had compassion on them and healed their sick. MATTHEW 14:14 NLT

What does that mean to me?

Because Jesus came to earth in the form of a human, He *totally* understands how you are feeling and what you are going through. So run to Him with all your troubles. He "gets" it! His shoulder is ready for you to cry on!

Law of Moses

What is the Law of Moses?

The first five books of the Bible written by Moses—Genesis, Exodus, Leviticus, Numbers, and Deuteronomy. It includes the Ten Commandments.

What is it all about?

The Law of Moses gave God's people lots of rules to obey to help people get right with God. But all these rules were really hard to follow. Then Jesus came along. Now "everyone who believes in him is declared right with God—something the law of Moses could never do" (Acts 13:39 NLT).

What is an important verse about the Law of Moses?

"I will put My Law into their minds. And I will write it on their hearts. I will be their God, and they will be My people."
JEREMIAH 31:33 NLV

What does that mean to me?

God's laws have been written on your heart. So you already know what is right and wrong. And you know the main rules to follow: love God, yourself, and your neighbor.

Fiery Furnace

What is the fiery furnace?

A really hot place where King Nebuchadnezzar sent three young men named Shadrach, Meshach, and Abednego.

What is it all about?

Shadrach, Meshach, and Abednego would not worship the king's golden statue, so they were thrown into the fiery furnace to die.

What is an important verse about the fiery furnace?

"Look!" Nebuchadnezzar shouted. "I see four men, unbound, walking around in the fire unharmed! And the fourth looks like a god!" DANIEL 3:25 NLT

What does that mean to me?

No matter what tight spot you get into, God will be in it with you. And He will make sure you get out with Him!

Olives

What are olives?

Large, black fruits that grow from the olive tree.

What is it all about?

The olive tree is very common in Israel. Its unripe fruit is green. About one-third of the olive fruit is oil. Olive oil is very valuable. The Israelites used the oil for cooking and anointing. Olive trees are very strong and sturdy.

What is an important verse about olives?

I am like an olive tree, thriving in the house of God.
I will always trust in God's unfailing love. PSALM 52:8 NLT

What does that mean to me?

Always trust Jesus. When you do, you will be as strong and sturdy as a happy and healthy olive tree. And you will bloom wherever you are planted!

Garden of Eden

What is the Garden of Eden?

The really wonderful place where God put Adam and Eve—the first man and woman on earth.

What is it all about?

Adam and Eve disobeyed God by eating fruit from the Tree of the Knowledge of Good and Evil. Afterward, God sent them out of the Garden.

What is an important verse about the Garden of Eden?

They will be permitted to enter through the gates of the city and eat the fruit from the tree of life. REVELATION 22:14 NLT

What does that mean to me?

God has angels and a flaming sword guarding the way to the Tree of Life. But someday believers will be let back into the Garden of Eden and live with God there. Now that's paradise!

Truth

What is truth?

What is actually true—whether a person likes it or not.

What is it all about?

Jesus said that He is "the Way and the Truth and the Life" (John 14:6 NLV). That means everything that He does and says is true! And whoever really wants to know the truth will listen to what He says.

What is an important verse about truth?

"When the Spirit of truth comes, he will guide you into all truth. He will not speak on his own but will tell you what he has heard." JOHN 16:13 NLT

What does that mean to me?

If you are ever not sure what is true and what is false, ask the Holy Spirit to help you figure it out. That's what He's here for! And He will never lead you astray.

Wisdom

What is wisdom?

The smarts that a person can only get from God.

What is it all about?

Wisdom is all about asking God for help when there are decisions to make. God helps people make up their minds and do the right thing. King Solomon asked God for wisdom. That pleased God so much that He gave Solomon money and power, too.

What is an important verse about wisdom?

If any of you need wisdom, ask God for it. He will give it to you. God gives freely to everyone. He doesn't find fault. JAMES 1:5

What does that mean to me?

Are you having trouble figuring something out? Are you not sure what you should do? Then run to God and ask Him for wisdom. He can't wait to give it to you!

Spiritual Gifts

What are spiritual gifts?

Talents God has given His people to serve Him, their family, church, and others.

What is it all about?

Spirituals gifts can be giving wise advice, having special knowledge and great faith, the gift of healing, doing miracles, predicting what's going to happen, helping others, and more (see 1 Corinthians 12:7–10)!

What is an important verse about spiritual gifts?

God has given each of you a gift from his great variety of spiritual gifts. Use them well to serve one another. 1 PETER 4:10 NLT

What does that mean to me?

Do you know what your spiritual gift is? If not, ask God to help you figure it out. Then find a way to use it for His glory!

Last Supper

What is the Last Supper?

The last meal Jesus and His disciples ate before He was killed.

What is it all about?

At this last meal at Passover, Jesus told His disciples that He would soon be betrayed by one of them and then killed. In memory of this night, today's believers celebrate *communion* by drinking a cup of juice made from grapes and eating some bread.

What is an important verse about the Last Supper?

A person should take a careful look at himself before he eats the bread and drinks from the cup. 1 CORINTHIANS 11:28

What does that mean to me?

Before you celebrate communion, make sure you are coming to God with a clean heart, a peaceful mind, and a humble spirit.

Loaves and Fishes

What are the loaves and fishes?

Over 5,000 people—men, women, and children—were fed with one small boy's five loaves of bread and two fishes.

What is it all about?

Jesus had been preaching to a big crowd of people. When dinner came, He didn't want to send them away hungry. So He blessed a boy's loaves and fishes—and was able to feed everyone!

What is an important verse about loaves and fishes?

They all ate as much as they wanted, and afterward, the disciples picked up twelve baskets of leftovers!
MATTHEW 14:20 NLT

What does that mean to me?

You have a God that will never let you go away empty. He can, will, and does take what little blessings you have and multiply them over and over again!

Manna

What is manna?

A kind of bread that God made.

What is it all about?

When the Israelites were out in the desert and very hungry, God rained down a special bread from heaven to feed them (see Exodus 16:4). They weren't sure what this stuff was so they called it *manna*, a Hebrew word that means "what is it?"

What is an important verse about manna?

Jesus said, "I am the bread of life. No one who comes to me will ever go hungry. And no one who believes in me will ever be thirsty." JOHN 6:35

What does that mean to me?

With Jesus in your life, you will never thirst or be hungry in spirit. He is your manna from heaven!

Salvation

What is salvation?

Being rescued from the power and punishment of sin.

What is it all about?

After Adam and Eve ate the fruit God told them *not* to eat, sin entered the world. And with sin came separation from God and others, death of the spirit, and judgment from God. But then Jesus died on the cross and rescued God's people. Now those who believe in Him are good with God and can live with Him now and forever! Jesus is a believer's salvation!

What is an important verse about salvation?

You have always obeyed God. . . . So continue to work out your own salvation. Do it with fear and trembling.
PHILIPPIANS 2:12

What does that mean to me?

Even though you are already saved, God wants you to use His power within you to love and obey Him—forever and today!

Parable

What is a parable?

A picture-story used to help people understand a truth.

What is it all about?

People love to hear stories and will pay attention to them. So Jesus told people dozens of parables (stories) to help explain His (and God's) ideas. Most of the parables were written down by Luke. All of them related to everyday things that people could understand. The most famous parables are the Good Samaritan, the Prodigal Son, and the Talents. Each one teaches a very important lesson.

What is an important verse about a parable?

Jesus said, "In what way can we show what the holy nation of God is like? Or what picture-story can we use to help you understand?" MARK 4:30 NLV

What does that mean to me?

If you want to really understand what Jesus is all about, read His parables. Then you will "get" His words—for sure! And that will make it even easier to share His lessons with others!

Second Coming

What is the Second Coming?

The time when Jesus comes back to earth.

What is it all about?

Jesus will return to finish the work He came to do—to save as many people as He can.

What is an important verse about the Second Coming?

Christ died once for all time as a sacrifice to take away the sins of many people. He will come again, not to deal with our sins, but to bring salvation to all who are eagerly waiting for him. HEBREWS 9:28 NLT

What does that mean to me?

No one knows when Jesus will come back. So don't worry about it. Instead, just keep living for and believing in God and doing good things. That way you'll always be ready!

Tabernacle

What is the Tabernacle?

A tent where God's children met Him in the early days of Israel's history.

What is it all about?

After Moses led the Israelites out of Egypt, he built the Tabernacle. Inside was put the ark of the covenant and special furniture and things used to worship God.

What is an important verse about the Tabernacle?

"Our ancestors carried the Tabernacle with them through the wilderness. It was constructed according to the plan God had shown to Moses." ACTS 7:44 NLT

What does that mean to me?

The Tabernacle used to be the place where a priest could meet God. Later, Jesus came along and made it so that you, a believer, can meet God anytime, anywhere! So, meet up with Him today!

Noah's Ark

What is Noah's Ark?

A really big boat that God told Noah to build.

What is it all about?

Thousands of years ago, people were behaving very badly. So God decided to flood them all out—except for Noah, his family, and two of each animal.

What is an important verse about Noah's Ark?

Noah had faith. . . . God had warned him about things that could not yet be seen. . . . Because of his faith he was considered right with God. HEBREWS 11:7

What does that mean to me?

Even though Noah did not see even one drop of rain, he still believed God enough to build the ark. Ask God what He wants *you* to believe—without first seeing.

Serpent

What is a serpent?

A snake. It's also a name for the devil or Satan, the father of lies.

What is it all about?

After a serpent tricked Eve into disobeying God in the Garden of Eden, she and Adam were kicked out of the garden. Jesus is the only one who can get people close to God again.

What is an important verse about a serpent?

I fear that somehow your pure and undivided devotion to Christ will be corrupted, just as Eve was deceived by the cunning ways of the serpent. 2 CORINTHIANS 11:3 NLT

What does that mean to me?

Don't be tricked into believing lies about God or Jesus. Instead, keep your mind and eyes on God and His Word, and all will be well!

Sheep

What are sheep?

Small, horned mammals raised for food and wool.

What is it all about?

In Israel, lots of people raised herds of sheep. These *shepherds* guarded their flocks day and night. People were often compared to sheep. Jesus called Himself the Good Shepherd. Believers are thought of as His flock.

What is an important verse about sheep?

"I am the Good Shepherd. I know My sheep and My sheep know Me. . . . My sheep hear My voice and I know them. They follow Me." JOHN 10:14, 27 NLV

What does that mean to me?

Jesus is always watching over you. He knows you, and you Him. You will know His voice when He speaks. Listen. . . . Then follow. He knows the best way.

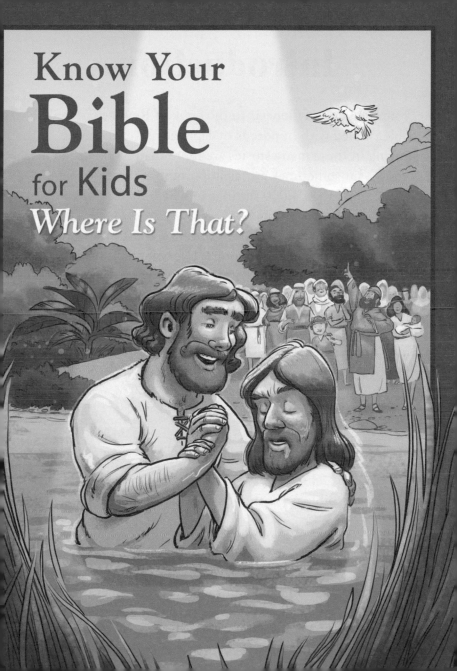

Know Your
Bible
for Kids
Where Is That?

Introduction

From the book of Genesis to the book of Revelation, the Bible is filled with hundreds of captivating stories. And starring in these many stories are more than 3,000 different people. But sometimes just as important as these people are the more than 1,000 settings in which their stories take place. In this unique book, *Know Your Bible for Kids— Where Is That?*, we have chosen 99 of the most interesting and important places in scripture. Every fascinating and illustrated sketch—from the miraculous water pile-up in the town of Adam to the never-ending flour and oil in the village of Zarephath—follows this outline:

• *Where is this place?*
A brief geographic description of the site mentioned in the Bible.

• *What's it all about?*
Details about what happened there.

• *What's an important verse about this place?*
A key Bible verse about that site.

• *What does that mean to me?*
What the history of this place teaches God's readers.

One of the great things about the Bible is the fact that we can learn so much about what happened where and with whom. As we imagine ourselves in each setting—even though it may still be shrouded in mystery or be in ruins today—that unique place, its history, its heroes, and God Himself come alive.

We hope you will use this fun, fascinating, and fact-filled book to better understand God's timeless lessons and realize that no matter where you are, God is always with you, guiding you today and into tomorrow.

Adam

Where is Adam?

This city was on the Jordan River.

What's it all about?

Joshua and the Israelites were trying to get into the land God had promised them. But first they had to cross the overflowing Jordan. The Lord told them that as soon as the priests carrying the Ark of God stepped into the river, the water would back up at the city of Adam and the people could cross.

What's an important verse about Adam?

Right away the water that was coming down the river stopped flowing. It piled up far away at a town called Adam near Zarethan. . . . So the people went across the Jordan River opposite Jericho. JOSHUA 3:16

What does that mean to me?

God will do amazing things to get you where He wants you to be.

Ai

Where is Ai?

Near the town of Jericho.

What's it all about?

The first time Joshua and the Israelites attacked this small village of Ai, they lost the battle. That's because after their earlier victory over Jericho, an Israelite named Achan had taken things that didn't belong to him. When Achan came clean with what he'd done, God gave Joshua a new battle plan and a promise.

What's an important verse about Ai?

"Do not be afraid or discouraged. Take all your fighting men and attack Ai, for I have given you the king of Ai, his people, his town, and his land." JOSHUA 8:1 NLT

What does that mean to me?

When you obey God, He is sure to help you win over your enemies.

Aijalon

Where is Aijalon?

On the boundary between the kingdoms of Judah and Israel.

What's it all about?

Joshua and the Israelites fought five kings and their armies who wanted to take over the town of Gibeon. To totally defeat his enemies, Joshua asked God to make the sun and moon stand still, giving him enough light to finish the job.

What's an important verse about Aijalon?

"Sun, stand still over Gibeon. Moon, stand still over the Valley of Aijalon." So the sun stood still. The moon stopped. They didn't move again until the nation won the battle over its enemies.
JOSHUA 10:12–13

What does that mean to me?

When you are working for God, He will listen to your prayers and move heaven and earth to help you.

Anab

Where is Anab?

In the mountains of Judah.

What's it all about?

Joshua and his great army fought many battles to win the Promised Land. During one of these fights, Joshua met up with a fierce race of giants.

What's an important verse about Anab?

Joshua went and killed the big powerful men in the hill country. He killed them in Hebron, Debir, Anab, and all the hill country of Judah and Israel.
JOSHUA 11:21 NLV

What does that mean to me?

God is big and mighty. He can take care of any giants you meet up with in life.

Antioch

Where is Antioch?

There are two places called Antioch. One is in Syria; the other was in Pisidia, the area of today's Turkey.

In Antioch, Syria, Jews let non-Jews into their church. In Antioch, Pisidia, Paul and Barnabas did a great job in telling the people about Jesus. But some people weren't happy about that, so Paul and Barnabas left the city.

What's an important verse about Antioch, Syria?

Many people put their trust in the Lord and turned to Him.... For a year they [Paul and Barnabas] taught many people in the church. The followers were first called Christians in Antioch [Syria]. ACTS 11:21, 26 NLV

What's an important verse about Antioch, Pisidia?

They worked against Paul and Barnabas and made them leave their city. But Paul and Barnabas shook the dust off from their feet against them [in Antioch, Pisidia] and went to the city of Iconium. ACTS 13:50–51 NLV

What does that mean to me?

When you are working for God, He finds a way to help you shake off defeat and live in victory!

Aphek

Near Jezreel in Israel.

What's it all about?

The Israelites were not obeying God very well. So they lost a battle with the Philistines. Afterward, the Israelites decided to take the Ark of God (which had the 10 Commandments in it) with its priests—Hophni and Phinehas—into the next battle. The Israelites thought it would help them win. It didn't. They lost the battle—*and more*!

What's an important verse about Aphek?

The Israelite army was camped near Ebenezer, and the Philistines were at Aphek. . . . The Ark of God was captured, and Hophni and Phinehas, the two sons of Eli, were killed. 1 SAMUEL 4:1, 11 NLT

What does that mean to me?

Things won't save you—but being right with God will!

Armageddon

Where is Armageddon?

A word that shows up only one time in the Bible, *Armageddon* means "the Mount of Megiddo." It could be a real place or just a word being used to describe a battlefield.

What's it all about?

Armageddon is where a final battle will be fought between Christ and all the wicked people on earth. Christ will win!

What's an important verse about Armageddon?

Then the evil spirits gathered the kings together. The place where the kings met is called Armageddon in the Hebrew language. REVELATION 16:16

What does that mean to me?

Nothing is stronger or more powerful than Jesus Christ. When you are on His side, you will always come out a winner!

Ashdod

Where is Ashdod?

This Philistine city is near the Mediterranean Sea.

What's it all about?

When the Philistines captured the Ark of God, the people of Ashdod put it in the temple of their god Dagon. The next morning, they found Dagon had fallen on its face. The day after that, things were worse!

What's an important verse about Ashdod?

The statue of Dagon. . .was, lying on the ground again! It had fallen on its face in front of the ark of the LORD. Its head and hands had been broken off. Only the body of the statue was left. 1 SAMUEL 5:4

What does that mean to me?

Be brave, because your God beats out all other gods— hands down!

Assyria

Where is Assyria?

Assyria was a country in the area of today's nations of Turkey and Iraq.

What's it all about?

Sennacherib, the king of Assyria, put his armies all around the city of Jerusalem. They were letting no food or water get through to King Hezekiah and his people. God's people were very hungry and thirsty. But Hezekiah came up with an idea!

What's an important verse about Assyria?

The rest of the events in Hezekiah's reign, including the extent of his power and how he built a pool and dug a tunnel to bring water into the city, are recorded.
2 KINGS 20:20 NLT

What does that mean to me?

When you are in a jam, God will either help you find a way out or bring His blessings in.

Athens

In today's country of Greece.

What's it all about?

All the latest ideas in books, plays, and beliefs were talked about in Athens. It was a center of great learning. There people worshipped lots of different idols made into statues.

What's an important verse about Athens?

While Paul was waiting for them [Silas and Timothy] in Athens, he was deeply troubled by all the idols he saw everywhere in the city. ACTS 17:16 NLT

What does that mean to me?

God is not something made by man's hands. He cannot be contained in clay. He is a spirit living inside of you. You can take Him everywhere you go! He's all you need to know!

Babel

Where is Babel?

This was the name of a tower and a city. The tower was built by ancient people in today's Syria after the Flood.

What's it all about?

Many years ago, everyone spoke the same language. The people began building a tower to reach heaven, to make a name for themselves. To bring them down to earth, God decided to stop their building and show them that *He* was the highest power.

What's an important verse about Babel?

So the name of the city was Babel, because there the Lord mixed up the language of the whole earth. The Lord sent the people everywhere over the whole earth.
GENESIS 11:9 NLV

What does that mean to me?

It's more important to make a name for God than for yourself.

Babylon

Where is Babylon?

An ancient kingdom, Babylon was in southern Mesopotamia.

What's it all about?

Babylon destroyed the nation of Judah, including Jerusalem and its temple, and carried the Israelites off to Babylon. That's where Daniel and his friends—Shadrach, Meshach, and Abednego—ended up. Those friends refused to worship the god of Nebuchadnezzar, king of Babylon, were thrown into a furnace, and lived to tell about it. And Daniel lived after being thrown into a den of lions!

What are some important verses about Babylon?

[King Nebuchadnezzar] carried away to Babylon those who had not been killed by the sword.
2 CHRONICLES 36:20 NLV

Nebuchadnezzar said, "Praise be to the God of Shadrach, Meshach, and Abed-nego. He has sent His angel and saved His servants who put their trust in Him."
DANIEL 3:28 NLV

What does that mean to me?

No matter where you go, God is with you. And, if you trust Him, He will always save you!

Bashan

Where is Bashan?

In the southern part of today's Syria.

What's it all about?

When Moses and the Israelites were wandering around in the desert, they came to the fruitful land of Bashan. Its ruler was King Og, a giant whose iron bed was more than 13 feet long and 6 feet wide.

What's an important verse about Bashan?

Og the king of Bashan went out with all his people to battle at Edrei. But the Lord said to Moses, "Do not be afraid of him. For I have given him into your hand." NUMBERS 21:33–34 NLV

What does that mean to me?

Don't let giants and bullies scare you. God is bigger than any of them.

Beer-Lahai-Roi

Where is Beer-Lahai-Roi?

Between the towns of Kadesh and Bered in Israel.

What's it all about?

Hagar, a slave woman, was pregnant with Abraham's baby. Abraham's childless wife, Sarah, started treating Hagar badly, so Hagar ran away. God found her by a spring of water. He told her to go back home.

What's an important verse about Beer-Lahai-Roi?

She called him "You are the God who sees me." . . . That's why the well was named Beer Lahai Roi. GENESIS 16:13 14

What does that mean to me?

God will always find you, no matter where you go. So you might as well stay right where you are. Tell Him your troubles. Then listen and obey—and all will be well!

Beer-Sheba

Where is Beer-Sheba?

In the Promised Land, southwest of the town Hebron.

What's it all about?

Abraham sent Hagar and their son Ishmael away with some food and water. They wandered in the desert of Beer-Sheba. After Hagar and Ishmael ran out of water, they sat down and cried. God heard them.

What's an important verse about Beer-Sheba?

God opened Hagar's eyes. She saw a well of water.
So she went and filled the bottle with water.
And she gave the boy a drink. GENESIS 21:19

What does that mean to me?

Always stay close to God. He will open your eyes so you can see all His blessings and have joy—even through your tears.

Bethany

Where is Bethany?

Near Jerusalem.

What's it all about?

Jesus' good friends Mary, Martha, and Lazarus lived in
Bethany. When Lazarus got sick, his sisters sent a message
for Jesus to come to Bethany. By the time He got there,
Lazarus had been dead for four days.

What's an important verse about Bethany?

Jesus arrived in Bethany, the home of Lazarus—the man
he had raised from the dead. A dinner was prepared in
Jesus' honor. Martha served, and Lazarus was among those
who ate with him. JOHN 12:1–2 NLT

What does that mean to me?

When you are in trouble, ask for Jesus. Then wait patiently.
He'll get to you—in *His* own *good* time!

Bethel

Where is Bethel?

About 11 miles north of Jerusalem.

What's it all about?

Bethel means "house of God." While running from his angry brother, Esau, Jacob stopped to sleep in Bethel. There he had a dream about a ladder reaching from earth into heaven. Angels were going up and down it. God was at the top of the ladder. He promised never to leave Jacob.

What are some important verses about Bethel?

Jacob woke up from his sleep. Then he thought, "The LORD is certainly in this place. And I didn't even know it.... This must be the house of God. This is the gate of heaven." GENESIS 28:16–17

Early the next morning Jacob took the stone he had placed under his head. He set it up as a pillar.... He named that place Bethel. GENESIS 28:18–19

What does that mean to me?

God is with you wherever you go—even in the most unusual places in heaven, on earth, and in between.

Bethlehem

Where is Bethlehem?

Five miles south of Jerusalem, Israel.

What's it all about?

Bethlehem is a very important city. That's because lots of good things happened there. It's where Ruth and Boaz, the great-grandparents of King David, met. That's where David was born—*and* where God said *Jesus* would be born!

What are some important verses about Bethlehem?

The LORD says, "Bethlehem, you might not be an important town in the nation of Judah. But out of you will come a ruler over Israel for me." MICAH 5:2

Jesus was born in Bethlehem in Judea. This happened while Herod was king of Judea. After Jesus' birth, Wise Men from the east came to Jerusalem. MATTHEW 2:1

What does that mean to me?

God had Jesus' birth, life, and death planned from the very beginning! So don't worry about what happened today or what is going to happen tomorrow. Just trust God. He's got a plan for you, too!

Bethsaida

Where is Bethsaida?

Northeast of the Sea of Galilee.

What's it all about?

Bethsaida means "house of the fisherman." Philip, Andrew, and Peter were from Bethsaida—and were fisherman! These ordinary people became extraordinary followers of a man named Jesus.

What's an important verse about Bethsaida?

The next day Jesus wanted to go to the country of Galilee. He found Philip and said to him, "Follow Me." Philip was from the town of Bethsaida. Andrew and Peter were from this town also.
JOHN 1:43–44 NLV

What does that mean to me?

God uses ordinary people to do extraordinary things. So get ready—God can equip you to do anything!

Caesarea

Where is Caesarea?

On the shore of the Mediterranean Sea, on the plain of Sharon.

What's it all about?

Cornelius, a Roman commander, was faithful to God. When Peter arrived and talked with Cornelius, the Holy Spirit appeared.

What's an important verse about Caesarea?

A man named Cornelius lived in Caesarea. . . . Some Jewish believers had come with Peter. They were amazed because the gift of the Holy Spirit had been poured out even on those who weren't Jews. ACTS 10:1, 45

What does that mean to me?

It doesn't matter if you are rich or poor, live in America or Europe. The power of the Holy Spirit is for anyone who believes. Do you believe?

Cana

Where is Cana?

In Galilee.

What's it all about?

Jesus, His followers, and His mother, Mary, went to a wedding in Cana. When they ran out of wine, Jesus turned some water into wine. And it was better than what they had been drinking before!

What's an important verse about Cana?

This was the first powerful work Jesus did. It was done in Cana of Galilee where He showed His power. His followers put their trust in Him.
JOHN 2:11 NLV

What does that mean to me?

Give all you have to Jesus—then trust Him to make it even better than before!

Canaan

Where is Canaan?

Also known as the Promised Land, it was west of the Jordan River.

What's it all about?

God told Abraham to leave his home and go to a land God would show him. Abraham had no idea where God was taking him, but he trusted God to keep His promise.

What's an important verse about Canaan?

The Lord said to Abram, "Leave your country, your family and your father's house, and go to the land that I will show you." . . . So they came to the land of Canaan.
GENESIS 12:1, 5 NLV

What does that mean to me?

Like Abraham, you, too, can trust God to lead you. Just step out—even though you might not know where you're headed—into His promise!

Capernaum

Where is Capernaum?

Near the Sea of Galilee.

What's it all about?

When Jesus began teaching in Nazareth, where He had grown up, the people did not accept Him. So, He decided to make Capernaum His home. He did many miracles there.

What are some important verses about Capernaum?

Jesus entered Capernaum again. The people heard that he had come home. So many people gathered that there was no room left. MARK 2:1–2

When Jesus entered Capernaum, a Roman commander came to him. . . . "Lord, I am not good enough to have you come into my house. But just say the word, and my servant will be healed." MATTHEW 8:5, 8

What does that mean to me?

Where you have faith, Jesus can do lots of miracles! So if you need help, run to Him. One word from His lips and all will be well!

City of David

Where is the City of David?

In Israel. This city was first called Jebus, then Jerusalem.

What's it all about?

When David became king, he wanted to make Jebus his capital. It was so well protected, he had trouble getting in. Then David found out the town had a water tunnel.

What's an important verse about the City of David?

The people living in the land. . .said to David, "You will not come here." . . . But David took the strong place of Zion, that is, the city of David. 2 SAMUEL 5:6–7 NLV

What does that mean to me?

When things seem impossible in your eyes, remember— they are not impossible with God.

Colosse

Where is Colosse?

In today's country of Turkey.

What's it all about?

While he was in prison, the apostle Paul wrote a letter to the people of the church in Colosse. The people there were listening to false teachers and moving away from Jesus. Paul's letter later became a Bible book called Colossians.

What's an important verse about Colosse?

We are writing to God's holy people in the city of Colosse, who are faithful brothers and sisters in Christ. May God our Father give you grace and peace.
COLOSSIANS 1:2 NLT

What does that mean to me?

Read and learn from the Word of God. Doing so will keep you close to Jesus' truth and God's power and strength.

Corinth

In the Roman area of Achaia, a western part of today's country of Greece.

The apostle Paul was a missionary. That means he traveled all over, talking about Jesus and setting up churches. One of the places Paul visited was Corinth. Later he wrote this church two letters. Both can be found in the Bible in books called First and Second Corinthians.

What are some important verses about Corinth?

Paul left Athens and went to Corinth.... Paul went to see Aquila and Priscilla. They were tentmakers, just as he was. So he stayed and worked with them. ACTS 18:1–3

Many others who lived in Corinth heard Paul.... One night the Lord spoke to Paul in a vision. "Don't be afraid," he said. "Keep on speaking. Don't be silent. I am with you." ACTS 18:8–10

What does that mean to me?

God gave Paul, a tentmaker, lots of courage. If you walk God's way, He'll give you courage, too!

Damascus

Where is Damascus?

In the country of Syria.

What's it all about?

Before becoming a Christian, the apostle Paul was called Saul. Saul was going around killing people who were following Jesus—that is, until Jesus stopped him with a bright light and a booming voice!

What's an important verse about Damascus?

On his journey, Saul approached Damascus. Suddenly a light from heaven flashed around him. He fell to the ground. He heard a voice speak to him.
Acts 9:3–4

What does that mean to me?

Sometimes God will stop you in your tracks. So keep your eyes and ears open to Him. Then listen carefully. God may be trying to tell you something.

Dead Sea

Where is the Dead Sea?

This lowest place on earth is a really big lake in Israel. It's also called the Salt Sea.

What's it all about?

The Dead Sea is four times saltier than the ocean. It's called the Dead Sea because fish can't live in its salty water. But the prophet Ezekiel had a fishy vision about it.

What's an important verse about the Dead Sea?

"The waters of this stream will make the salty waters of the Dead Sea fresh and pure. There will be swarms of living things wherever the water of this river flows. Fish will abound in the Dead Sea." EZEKIEL 47:8–9 NLT

What does that mean to me?

If you need a fresh start, go to God. He'll help you feel like new!

Derbe

Where is Derbe?

Derbe was in an area called Galatia, which is in today's country of Turkey.

What's it all about?

The apostle Paul stopped here last on his first missionary trip, and first on his second journey.

What's an important verse about Derbe?

Some Jews. . .turned the minds of the people against Paul and Barnabas and told them to throw stones at Paul. . . . They dragged him out of the city thinking he was dead. As the Christians gathered around Paul, he got up and went back into the city. The next day he went with Barnabas to Derbe. ACTS 14:19–20 NLV

What does that mean to me?

God wants believers to help other believers get to a safe place. Who can you "gather around" today?

Ebenezer

Near Mizpah in Israel.

What's it all about?

Samuel, a prophet of God, told the Israelites that if they worshiped only the Lord, they would win the next battle over the Philistines. So the Israelites put away their strange gods—and won the battle!

What's an important verse about Ebenezer?

Then Samuel took a stone and set it between Mizpah and Shen. He gave it the name Ebenezer, saying, "The Lord has helped us this far."
1 SAMUEL 7:12 NLV

What does that mean to me?

God is the only one true god who can truly help you. So look to Him—and no one else—for every victory!

Eden, Garden of

Where is the Garden of Eden?

Somewhere along the Tigris and Euphrates rivers in Mesopotamia.

What's it all about?

God put the first two humans—Adam and Eve—in a wonderful garden where they could live in peace and talk with Him every day. But then a snake tempted Adam and Eve to disobey God. So He sent them out of Eden for good.

What's an important verse about the Garden of Eden?

Eve was fooled by the snake in the garden of Eden. In the same way, I am afraid that you will be fooled and led away from your pure love for Christ. 2 CORINTHIANS 11:3 NLV

What does that mean to me?

Don't let anyone fool you into turning away from Jesus. Sticking with Him is your only chance at paradise.

Egypt

Where is Egypt?

On the northern tip of the continent of Africa.

What's it all about?

Sometimes during days of no rain, God's people went to Egypt for food and water. Israel's son Joseph became a powerful leader there. But after he died, the Egyptians made the Israelites their slaves.

What's an important verse about Egypt?

The Lord said [to Moses from a burning bush], "I have seen the suffering of My people in Egypt. I have heard their cry. . . . I know how they suffer. So I have come down to save them." EXODUS 3:7–8 NLV

What does that mean to me?

God knows what is happening in your life. He hears your cries. He will save you!

Elah Valley

Where is the Elah Valley?

About 15 miles from Bethlehem, Israel.

What's it all about?

In the Elah Valley, King Saul and his soldiers, including the older brothers of a shepherd boy named David, were being teased by a Philistine giant named Goliath. David bravely faced this giant with a simple slingshot and five smooth stones.

What's an important verse about the Elah Valley?

The religious leader said, "The sword is here that belonged to Goliath the Philistine, whom you killed in the valley of Elah." . . . And David said, "There is none like it. Give it to me." 1 SAMUEL 21:9 NLV

What does that mean to me?

No matter how young you are, God can give you the courage to face giants!

Emmaus

Where is Emmaus?

About seven miles from Jerusalem, Israel.

What's it all about?

After Jesus died on the cross, He was buried. Two of His followers, walking on the road to Emmaus, were sad that He was gone. But then He appeared right next to them. When they realized who He was, He disappeared again!

What's an important verse about Emmaus?

The two from Emmaus told their story of how Jesus had appeared to them as they were walking along the road, and how they had recognized him as he was breaking the bread. And just as they were telling about it, Jesus himself was suddenly standing there among them.
LUKE 24:35–36 NLT

What does that mean to me?

Jesus will always pop up—just when you need Him!

Endor

Where is Endor?

About four miles south of Mount Tabor in Israel.

What's it all about?

King Saul chased all the mediums (people who claim to get advice from the spirits of dead people) out of Israel. But then, facing a really big army, Saul became scared and too impatient to wait for God's guidance. So, through a medium, he sought advice from the dead prophet Samuel, who told Saul *he'd* die the next day—and Saul did!

What's an important verse about Endor?

Saul then said to his advisers, "Find a woman who is a medium, so I can go and ask her what to do." His advisers replied, "There is a medium at Endor."
1 SAMUEL 28:7 NLT

What does that mean to me?

Need some wisdom? Wait for *God's* advice. He always knows best!

En-Gedi

Where is En-Gedi?

This oasis called the "spring of the young goat" is on the western side of the Dead Sea.

What's it all about?

King Saul wanted to kill David. While looking for him in En-Gedi, Saul went into a cave. David turned out to be in there. He could've killed Saul—but he didn't. And God rewarded David for it.

What's an important verse about En-Gedi?

After Saul returned from fighting the Philistines, he was told that David had gone into the wilderness of En-gedi. So Saul. . .went to search for David and his men near the rocks of the wild goats. 1 SAMUEL 24:1–2 NLT

What does that mean to me?

God will reward you when you are kind to people who haven't been kind to you.

Ephesus

Where is Ephesus?

The ruins of this once-great city are in Turkey. The apostle Paul's letter to the church in Ephesus, the book of Ephesians, is in the Bible. Revelation 2 also mentions the church of Ephesus.

What's it all about?

In the name of Jesus, seven sons of Sceva, a chief Jewish priest, were driving demons out of people—until a man with an evil spirit jumped on all seven and left them naked and wounded!

What's an important verse about Ephesus?

All through Ephesus. . .fear descended on the city, and the name of the Lord Jesus was greatly honored. Many who became believers confessed their sinful practices.
ACTS 19:17–18 NLT

What does that mean to me?

Jesus' name is powerful—and only to be used by believers with a clean heart!

Galatia

This Roman region is in today's country of Turkey.

What's it all about?

The apostle Paul and Silas journeyed to Galatia on their first missionary trip. Later, Paul wrote to the believers in Galatia. The letter can be found in the Bible book Galatians.

What's an important verse about Galatia?

Paul and Silas traveled through the area of Phrygia and Galatia, because the Holy Spirit had prevented them from preaching the word in the province of Asia at that time. ACTS 16:6 NLT

What does that mean to me?

Sometimes you need to make sure your plans are the same as God's. So before doing anything, check in with Him. He'll let you know which path to take.

Galilee

Where is Galilee?

In northern Israel. The towns of Nazareth, Capernaum, Bethsaida, and Cana are all in Galilee.

What's it all about?

Jesus, the women who supported Him, and eleven of His disciples—all but Judas Iscariot—were from towns in Galilee. It's also where Jesus did most of His miracles.

What are some important verses about Galilee?

There will be a time in the future when Galilee of the Gentiles...will be filled with glory. The people who walk in darkness will see a great light. ISAIAH 9:1–2 NLT

"Men of Galilee," they said, "why are you standing here staring into heaven? Jesus has been taken from you into heaven, but someday he will return from heaven in the same way you saw him go!" ACTS 1:10–11 NLT

What does that mean to me?

God wants you to stay in the light of Jesus. You can do that by following His rule to love God, yourself, and everyone around you. So shine on! Jesus will be back soon!

Gath

Somewhere along the Mediterranean Sea in Israel.

What's it all about?

Goliath, the giant the scrawny little shepherd boy David killed with one stone, was from Gath.

What's an important verse about Gath?

A mighty hero named Goliath came out of the Philistine camp. He was from Gath. He was more than nine feet tall. He had a bronze helmet on his head. He wore a coat of bronze armor. It weighed 125 pounds. On his legs he wore bronze guards. He carried a bronze javelin on his back. His spear was as big as a weaver's rod. Its iron point weighed 15 pounds. 1 Samuel 17:4–7

What does that mean to me?

Remember to always count on God's strength—not your own! And giants will fall!

Gaza

Where is Gaza?

In today's Palestine.

What's it all about?

Gaza was a Philistine town. After evil Delilah had strongman Samson's hair cut off, the Philistines took the now-weak man to a prison in Gaza. Later, Samson's hair grew back, his God and strength returned, and by his death many Philistines were killed.

What's an important verse about Gaza?

He did not know that the Lord had left him. The Philistines took hold of him and cut out his eyes. They brought him down to Gaza and tied him with brass chains. Samson was made to grind grain in the prison.
JUDGES 16:20–21 NLV

What does that mean to me?

If you stay close to God, He will stay close to you.

Gethsemane

Where is Gethsemane?

This olive-tree grove is just a little way up the Mount of Olives in Jerusalem, Israel.

What's it all about?

After they ate the Last Supper, Jesus and His disciples
went to the Garden of Gethsemane. He told them to stay
awake and watch while He prayed. Jesus knew it was the
night before He would be killed.

What's an important verse about Gethsemane?

Jesus came with them to a place called Gethsemane.
He said to them, "You sit here while I go over there to
pray." He took Peter and the two sons of Zebedee with
Him. He began to have much sorrow and a heavy heart. . . .
He went on a little farther and got down with His face on
the ground. He prayed. MATTHEW 26:36–37, 39 NLV

What does that mean to me?

When you are troubled, follow Jesus' example. Ask some
friends to pray for you—or with you. Then go off by
yourself and have a secret talk with God. He'll help you.

Gilead

Where is Gilead?

East of the Jordan River, in today's country of Jordan.

What's it all about?

Jephthah promised to give God something—if God would help him win a battle. Jephthah won the fight—but lost his only daughter, who came out to greet him afterward.

What's an important verse about Gilead?

[Jephthah] passed through Gilead. . . . Jephthah made a promise to the Lord and said, "You give the people of Ammon into my hand. And I will give to the Lord whatever comes out of the doors of my house to meet me." JUDGES 11:29–31 NLV

What does that mean to me?

You don't need to make deals with God to get Him on your side. He's already there!

Gilgal

Where is Gilgal?

A Hebrew word meaning "circle," Gilgal was a town near Jericho.

What's it all about?

Joshua and the Israelites had to cross the flooding Jordan River to get to Gilgal, then Jericho. God helped them by stopping the water from flowing.

What's an important verse about Gilgal?

Joshua set up at Gilgal the twelve stones they had taken from the Jordan. . . . "Your children will ask their fathers some time in the future, 'What do these stones mean?' Then let your children know that Israel crossed this Jordan on dry ground." JOSHUA 4:20–22 NLV

What does that mean to me?

Find a way to mark how God blesses your life. Then see how many "stones" you end up with!

Golgotha

Where is Golgotha?

In ancient days, Golgotha was just outside of Jerusalem.
Today Golgotha is inside Jerusalem's walls.

What's it all about?

Golgotha is where Jesus was crucified on the cross along with two thieves. It was there that He died for our sins.

What's an important verse about Golgotha?

Carrying the cross by himself, he went to the place called Place of the Skull (in Hebrew, *Golgotha*). There they nailed him to the cross. . . . Jesus knew that his mission was now finished. . . . He said, "It is finished!" Then he bowed his head and released his spirit. JOHN 19:17–18, 28, 30 NLT

What does that mean to me?

Jesus finished His work on earth by dying on the cross for each one of us—and then rising again. But you are just beginning your work. What will you do for Jesus?

Gomorrah

Where is Gomorrah?

Either near or under the Dead Sea.

What's it all about?

Along with its sister city of Sodom in the valley, Gomorrah was full of people who behaved very badly. The city and all its people were destroyed, except for all of Lot's family. Well, almost all. . .

What's an important verse about Gomorrah?

The LORD sent down burning sulfur. It came down like rain on Sodom and Gomorrah. It came from the LORD out of the sky. He destroyed those cities and the whole valley. . . . But Lot's wife looked back. When she did, she became a pillar made out of salt. GENESIS 19:24–26

What does that mean to me?

When God gets you out of trouble, never look back. Just keep moving forward. . .with Him.

Harod Spring

Where is Harod Spring?

In northern Israel.

What's it all about?

Harod means "trembling." At this spring, God told Gideon he had too many soldiers. So Gideon first got rid of men who were afraid, then those who drank water by putting their mouths in the spring instead of cupping it in their hands. So instead of winning the battle with 32,000 soldiers, Gideon won with 300!

What's an important verse about Harod Spring?

Gideon. . .went as far as the spring of Harod. . . . The LORD said to Gideon, "If I let all of you fight the Midianites, the Israelites will boast to me that they saved themselves by their own strength." JUDGES 7:1–2 NLT

What does that mean to me?

God is the one who gives you the strength to win!

Heaven

Where is heaven?

Somewhere in the sky.

What's it all about?

After Jesus died, He rose up from the grave. Then He talked to His followers, and He rose up to heaven. That's where He hangs out now with God!

What's an important verse about heaven?

Then I saw a new heaven and a new earth. . . . "Look, God's home is now among his people! He will live with them, and they will be his people. God himself will be with them. He will wipe every tear from their eyes, and there will be no more death or sorrow or crying or pain." REVELATION 21:1, 3–4 NLT

What does that mean to me?

Someday you, as a believer, will live with God in heaven!

Hebron

Where is Hebron?

About 20 miles south of Jerusalem in today's West Bank.

What's it all about?

One day Abraham and his nephew split up. Lot went to the Jordan valley. Abraham went to Hebron.

What's an important verse about Hebron?

"Rise up and walk far and wide upon the land. For I will give it to you." Then Abram moved his tent and came to live among the oaks of Mamre in Hebron. There he built an altar to the Lord. GENESIS 13:17–18 NLV

What does that mean to me?

God loves grateful people. What can you do today as a way to thank Him for what He's given you?

Hell

Where is hell?

A place of much suffering because God isn't there.

What's it all about?

Jesus tells a story about a rich man who had everything but never gave anything to the beggar Lazarus. When both men died, the rich man went to hell and Lazarus to heaven. Between the two places, there was a very big space.

What's an important verse about hell?

"In hell. . .the rich man called out, 'Father Abraham! Have pity on me! Send Lazarus to dip the tip of his finger in water. Then he can cool my tongue with it. I am in terrible pain in this fire.'" LUKE 16:23–24

What does that mean to me?

Stick close to God on earth and you will be cool with Him in heaven!

Iconium

Where is Iconium?

In today's country of Turkey.

What's it all about?

Paul and Barnabas bravely went to Iconium and preached about Jesus. Afterward, some people decided to attack them. The two followers found out about the plan and ran away to preach in other places.

What's an important verse about Iconium?

Paul and Barnabas went to the Jewish synagogue [in Iconium] and preached with such power that a great number of both Jews and Greeks became believers.... And the Lord proved their message was true by giving them power to do miraculous signs. ACTS 14:1, 3 NLT

What does that mean to me?

When you tell people the truth about God, He backs you up in amazing ways.

Israel

In the Middle East, on the eastern shore of the Mediterranean Sea.

What's it all about?

Jacob, afraid and alone, prayed to God. Then he wrestled a blessing from a strange man. The man renamed Jacob *Israel*, which means "struggle with God." Later, Jacob's 12 sons got a part of the Promised Land called Israel.

What are some important verses about Israel?

Jacob said, "I will not let you go unless you bless me.".... "Your name will no longer be Jacob," the man told him. "From now on you will be called Israel, because you have fought with God and...won." GENESIS 32:26, 28 NLT

"I will give you the land I once gave to Abraham and Isaac. Yes, I will give it to you and your descendants after you." GENESIS 35:12 NLT

What does that mean to me?

No matter what fix you are in, pray to God. And hold on until He blesses you!

Jabbok River

Where is the Jabbok River?

Near Amman, the capital of today's country of Jordan.

What's it all about?

Some angels greeted Jacob when he neared the Jabbok River. So he camped there. Later he sent many animals across the Jabbok River. They were gifts he hoped would take the sting out of his brother Esau's anger. Later he wrestled with God—and won!

What's an important verse about the Jabbok River?

That night Jacob. . .took his two wives, his two female servants and his 11 sons and sent them across the Jabbok River. After they had crossed the stream, he sent over everything he owned. GENESIS 32:22–23

What does that mean to me?

Sometimes you need to empty your hands to get a good grip on God.

Jericho

Where is Jericho?

On the west side of the Jordan River.

What's it all about?

This is the first city Joshua and the Israelites won in battle as they went in to conquer the Promised Land. They marched around the city for six days. On the seventh, they shouted and Jericho's walls came down!

What's an important verse about Jericho?

The LORD said to Joshua, "I have given you Jericho, its king, and all its strong warriors. You and your fighting men should march around the town."
JOSHUA 6:2–3 NLT

What does that mean to me?

God has battles won before you even begin to fight! Sounds confusing—but it's true! So be brave. With God, anything can happen!

Jerusalem

Where is Jerusalem?

Once called Jebus and the City of David, this hilltop town is in Israel.

What's it all about?

David conquered Jerusalem and made it his capital. This is where David's son Solomon built God's temple, Jesus died on the cross, and His disciples received the Holy Spirit! Jerusalem has been conquered many times and destroyed at least five times.

What are some important verses about Jerusalem?

Pray for peace in Jerusalem. O Jerusalem, may there be peace within your walls and prosperity in your palaces.
PSALM 122: 6–7 NLT

[Jesus said,] "Do not leave Jerusalem until the Father sends you the gift he promised, as I told you before. . . . In just a few days you will be baptized with the Holy Spirit."
ACTS 1:4–5 NLT

What does that mean to me?

World peace begins with you, right where you are. So be a child of peace. Ask Jesus and the Holy Spirit to help you.

Jezreel Valley

Where is the Jezreel Valley?

In northern Israel.

What's it all about?

Many battles were fought in the Jezreel Valley. The Philistines gathered here to fight King Saul, his sons, and their army. Even though Saul had once tried to kill him, King David wrote a song of sadness about Saul and his son Jonathan dying in the Jezreel Valley.

What's an important verse about the Jezreel Valley?

When the Israelites on the other side of the Jezreel Valley and beyond the Jordan saw that the Israelite army had fled and that Saul and his sons were dead, they abandoned their towns and fled. So the Philistines moved in and occupied their towns. 1 SAMUEL 31:7 NLT

What does that mean to me?

God wants us all to be forgiving. . .like David was toward Saul.

Joppa

About 35 miles from Jerusalem. Today Joppa is the city called Jaffa.

What's it all about?

A believer named Tabitha (or Dorcas) lived in Joppa. She was a very good and kind woman who made clothes for others. When she got sick and died, her friends asked Peter to come right away. Peter came, prayed, then told Tabitha to get up. And she did!

What's an important verse about Joppa?

He gave her to them, a living person. News of this went through all Joppa. Many people put their trust in the Lord. ACTS 9:41–42 NLV

What does that mean to me?

God does amazing things for good and kind people. Who can you be kind to today?

Jordan River

Where is the Jordan River?

In Israel.

What's it all about?

Naaman the leper was a captain in the Syrian army. The prophet Elisha in Israel told him what to do to be healed. Eight hundred years later, Jesus was baptized in the Jordan River, right before defeating the devil in the desert.

What are some important verse about the Jordan

Naaman went down into the Jordan River seven times, as the man of God had told him. And his flesh was made as well as the flesh of a little child. . . . "Now I know that there is no God in all the earth but in Israel."
2 KINGS 5:14–15 NLV

Jesus was full of the Holy Spirit when He returned from the Jordan River. Then He was led by the Holy Spirit to a desert. LUKE 4:1 NLV

What does that mean to me?

Rivers are wonderful to take a dip in. But your real power comes from God's Holy Spirit! So why not take a dip in God's Word and be led by the Spirit today?

Judah

Where is Judah?

Judah was at first part of the country of Israel. But then the tribes of Israel had a disagreement. So they split. Judah became one country and Israel another. Today Judah is part of southern Israel.

The country of Judah was named after a son of Jacob (who was later named Israel). It was in Judah that King David and Jesus, members of the tribe of Judah, were born.

God said to him, "Speak to Solomon's son Rehoboam, the king of Judah. Speak to the royal house of Judah and Benjamin. Also speak to the rest of the people. Tell all of them, 'The LORD says, "Do not go up to fight against the Israelites. They are your relatives. I want every one of you to go back home. Things have happened exactly the way I planned them."'" 1 KINGS 12:22–24

No matter who splits from or argues with whom, be at peace. God has a plan!

Kadesh-Barnea

Where is Kadesh-Barnea?

About 90 miles south of Jerusalem, Israel.

What's it all about?

Moses sent 12 tribesmen to scope out Canaan. When they got back, all but Caleb and Joshua scared the people with tales of giants. And all but Caleb and Joshua died during the 40 years of desert wandering.

What's an important verse about Kadesh-Barnea?

Caleb. . .said. . ."I was forty years old when the Lord's servant Moses sent me from Kadesh-barnea to spy out the land. . . . My brothers who went up with me made the heart of the people weak with fear. But I followed the Lord my God with all my heart."
JOSHUA 14:6–8 NLV

What does that mean to me?

Don't follow fear—follow God with all your heart!

Kishon River

Where is the Kishon River?

In the Jezreel Valley in Israel.

What's it all about?

Deborah led the Israelite troops and their army commander, Barak, against attacks by an enemy king and his 900 charioteers. She helped Barak be brave by telling him God was going to hand the charioteers over to him. That's when sudden rain turned the dry Kishon riverbed into a fast-flowing river and swept away or trapped the charioteers in mud.

What's an important verse about the Kishon River?

Barak chased Sisera's chariots and army. . . . All of Sisera's men were killed with swords. Not even one was left.
JUDGES 4:16

What does that mean to me?

Stick with God's people. They—and God—will give you courage.

Laodicea

Where is Laodicea?

In today's western Turkey.

What's it all about?

In the Bible book of Revelation, Jesus told the church in Laodicea that its members were neither hot nor cold for Him, so He was going to spit them out of His mouth.

What's an important verse about Laodicea?

"Here I am! I stand at the door and knock. If any of you hears my voice and opens the door, I will come in and eat with you. And you will eat with me."
REVELATION 3:20

What does that mean to me?

When you are hot for Jesus and open the door to let Him in, His presence will shine even brighter in you!

Malta

Where is Malta?

In the Mediterranean Sea, south of Italy.

What's it all about?

The prisoner Paul was being taken by ship to Rome to stand trial when the ship ran into a very large storm. The ship wrecked on the island of Malta where Paul got bitten by a poisonous snake—and lived. Later, Paul healed the Maltese leader and other islanders.

What's an important verse about Malta?

Once we were safe on shore, we learned that we were on the island of Malta. The people of the island were very kind to us. ACTS 28:1–2 NLT

What does that mean to me?

Good things happen when you are kind to others—even when you are having troubles of your own.

Marah

Where is Marah?

In the wilderness of Etham, which was somewhere in northeastern Egypt.

What's it all about?

Three days after Moses led God's people through the Rea Sea, they stopped at Marah. They were very thirsty but couldn't drink the water. After crying out to God, Moses was shown a piece of wood. He threw it into the water and God made it okay to drink!

What's an important verse about Marah?

When they came to the oasis of Marah, the water was too bitter to drink. So they called the place Marah (which means "bitter"). EXODUS 15:23 NLT

What does that mean to me?

When you trust in God as your one and only master and miracle-maker, everything in life becomes sweet.

Midian

Where is Midian?

Some people think it's in Saudi Arabia.

What's it all about?

After killing an Egyptian for beating a Hebrew slave, Moses ran off to Midian. There he met his wife, shepherded sheep, and talked to God in a burning bush. Later, Moses led God's people out of Egypt.

What's an important verse about Midian?

Before Moses left Midian, the LORD said to him, "Return to Egypt, for all those who wanted to kill you have died." So Moses. . .headed back to the land of Egypt. In his hand he carried the staff of God. EXODUS 4:19–20 NLT

What does that mean to me?

God will give you everything you need to serve Him.

Moab

Where is Moab?

In today's country of Jordan.

What's it all about?

Moab, the son of Lot, and Lot's oldest daughter settled east of Israel. These Moabites became enemies of Israel. Many years later, Naomi, her husband, and her two sons moved to Moab because of a drought. Later, back in Israel, Naomi's widowed daughter-in-law Ruth married Boaz. They had a son named Obed, who became the grandfather of King David.

What's an important verse about Moab?

Naomi returned. And her daughter-in-law Ruth, the Moabite woman, returned with her from the land of Moab. They came to Bethlehem. RUTH 1:22 NLV

What does that mean to me?

God can use anything and anyone—even a drought, death, and a so-called enemy—to make good things happen!

Mount Carmel

Where is Mount Carmel?

In northern Israel.

What's it all about?

Elijah had a contest with priests who followed a false god that must have been traveling or asleep—because it didn't respond to the priests' prayers. But the one true God proved Himself by answering Elijah's prayer with fire.

What's an important verse about Mount Carmel?

Men who speak for the false gods [were] together at Mount Carmel. Elijah came near all the people and said, "How long will you be divided between two ways of thinking? If the Lord is God, follow Him. But if Baal is God, then follow him." 1 KINGS 18:20–21 NLV

What does that mean to me?

Follow God with your whole heart. Know that He's always around and awake, working things out for you.

Mount Nebo

Where is Mount Nebo?

East of the Jordan River in today's country of Jordan.

What's it all about?

Moses had led God's people to the Promised Land. When they got there, Moses went up Mount Nebo and God showed him the land. Then Moses got to go even higher—to heaven with God!

What's an important verse about Mount Nebo?

Moses went up from the valleys of Moab to Mount Nebo . . . . And the Lord showed him all the land. . . . Moses the servant of the Lord died. . . . And He buried him.
DEUTERONOMY 34:1, 5–6 NLV

What does that mean to me?

The nearer you get to God, the closer you'll get to heaven—in this life and the next!

Mount of Beatitudes

Where is the Mount of Beatitudes?

Somewhere in Israel.

What's it all about?

On the Mount of Beatitudes, Jesus taught the people how they should "be" to be blessed or happy. The word *beatitudes*, which does not show up in the Bible, comes from the Latin word *beatitudo*, which means "blessedness."

What's an important verse about the Mount of Beatitudes?

Jesus went up on the mountainside and sat down. His disciples gathered around him, and he began to teach them. "God blesses those who are. . ."
MATTHEW 5:1–3 NLT

What does that mean to me?

When you follow Jesus' beatitudes (listed in Matthew 5:3–11), you will be a happy dude with a good attitude!

Mount of Olives

Where is the Mount of Olives?

One mile from Jerusalem in Israel.

Jesus often spent time on the Mount of Olives, alone with God. That gave Jesus the energy to come down the hillside to heal, teach, and preach to the people. It's also the place where He prayed before being arrested—and where He rose to heaven.

What are some important verses about the Mount of Olives?

Each day Jesus taught at the temple. And each evening he went to spend the night on the hill called the Mount of Olives. LUKE 21:37

"Men of Galilee," they said, "why do you stand here looking at the sky? Jesus has been taken away from you into heaven. But he will come back in the same way you saw him go." The apostles returned to Jerusalem from the Mount of Olives. ACTS 1:11–12

What does that mean to me?

When you spend time alone with God, He will give you the power to do anything—and everything!

Mount Sinai (or Horeb)

Where is Mount Sinai?

Probably on Egypt's Sinai Peninsula.

What's it all about?

Mount Sinai is the place where God met with people. He met Moses there two times. The first time, Moses was shepherding his sheep at the mountain's bottom. The second time, he was shepherding people and met God at the mountaintop.

What are some important verses about Mount Sinai?

He led the flock to the west side of the desert, and came to Horeb, the mountain of God. There the Angel of the Lord showed Himself to Moses in a burning fire from inside a bush. EXODUS 3:1–2 NLV

The LORD finished speaking to Moses on Mount Sinai. Then he gave him the two tablets of the covenant. They were made out of stone. The words on them were written by the finger of God. EXODUS 31:18

What does that mean to me?

God will always find a way to get a message to His people. Are your eyes and ears open?

Nazareth

Where is Nazareth?

In Galilee, in today's Israel.

What's it all about?

Nazareth was Jesus' hometown. Because the people there only knew Him as the son of Joseph the carpenter, they turned away from the grown-up Jesus who came to preach, teach, and heal others. After He went to heaven, people on earth healed others in His name.

What are some important verses about Nazareth?

Jesus left there and went to his hometown of Nazareth . . . . Jesus laid his hands on a few sick people and healed them. But he could not do any other miracles there. He was amazed because they had no faith.
MARK 6:1, 5–6

Peter said, "I don't have any silver or gold. But I'll give you what I have. In the name of Jesus Christ of Nazareth, get up and walk." ACTS 3:6

What does that mean to me?

To see powerful miracles being done in Jesus' name, you have to believe He is more than just a man from Nazareth. He is God's Son.

New Jerusalem

Where is the New Jerusalem?

Some think it is heaven. Others say it's truly going to be a city that comes down from heaven.

What's it all about?

The Bible book Revelation says that God's people will one day live in a New Jerusalem. It will have streets of gold, where there will be no more pain or sorrow.

What's an important verse about the New Jerusalem?

And I saw the holy city, the new Jerusalem, coming down from God out of heaven.
REVELATION 21:2 NLT

What does that mean to me?

It doesn't really matter if the New Jerusalem is heaven or an actual new place on earth. What matters is that you, as a believer, will get to see it!

Nineveh

Where is Nineveh?

Near today's city of Mosul, Iraq.

What's it all about?

God told the prophet Jonah to go to the people of
Nineveh and tell them their city was going to be destroyed.
But Jonah didn't think the people would like that message.
So he went the other way. After Jonah spent some time
in the belly of a big fish, God asked him to go to Nineveh
again.

What's an important verse about Nineveh?

This time Jonah obeyed the LORD's command and went to
Nineveh, a city so large that it took three days to see it all.
JONAH 3:3 NLT

What does that mean to me?

It's always better to obey God—it keeps you from having a
whale of a bad time!

Ophrah

In central Israel.

What's it all about?

A man named Gideon lived in Ophrah. Before he had even thought about becoming a warrior for God, an angel told him, "The Lord is with you, O powerful soldier" (Judges 6:12 NLV).

What's an important verse about Ophrah?

The Lord said to him, "Peace be with you. Do not be afraid. You will not die." Then Gideon built an altar there to the Lord. He gave it the name, The Lord is Peace. It is still in Ophrah. JUDGES 6:23–24 NLV

What does that mean to me?

Never worry about who you will be. Just worship God— and He'll give you the strength to be that special person He knows you already are!

Paradise

Where is Paradise?

In God's perfect garden.

What's it all about?

Adam and Eve lived in a wonderful garden. There was no evil or death in it. Every day they walked and talked with God. But when they disobeyed God, they were sent out of Paradise.

What's an important verse about Paradise?

"Anyone with ears to hear must listen to the Spirit and understand what he is saying to the churches. To everyone who is victorious I will give fruit from the tree of life in the paradise of God." REVELATION 2:7 NLT

What does that mean to me?

If you stick with Jesus and walk like He walked, you will someday be with God in Paradise!

Patmos

Where is Patmos?

Off the coast of today's country of Turkey.

What's it all about?

As punishment for talking to people about Jesus, John was sent away to the small island of Patmos. There he had a vision. He wrote down everything he saw. It is in the Bible book called Revelation.

What's an important verse about Patmos?

I, John, am a believer like you. I am a friend who suffers like you. As members of Jesus' royal family, we can put up with anything that happens to us. I was on the island of Patmos because I taught God's word and what Jesus said.
REVELATION 1:9

What does that mean to me?

With Jesus, God's royal Son, as your Friend and Brother, you can get through anything!

Pergamum

Where is Pergamum?

In today's western Turkey.

What's it all about?

In the Bible book Revelation, Jesus had some words to say to seven churches. One of those seven was in Pergamum. Members of that church were following teachers who were leading them into doing wrong things.

What's an important verse about Pergamum?

"Here is what I command you to write to the church in Pergamum. . . . 'I have a few things against you. You have people there who follow the teaching of Balaam.'"
REVELATION 2:12, 14

What does that mean to me?

God wants you—and everyone at your church—to be following His teachings only. Then you will be doing the right things.

Persia

Where is Persia?

In today's country of Iran.

What's it all about?

At one time, Cyrus, a powerful ruler from Persia, defeated the country of Babylon and freed the Jewish people who had been sent there.

What's an important verse about Persia?

This is what King Cyrus of Persia says: "The LORD, the God of heaven, has given me all the kingdoms of the earth. He has appointed me to build him a Temple at Jerusalem, which is in Judah. Any of you who are the LORD's people may go there for this task. And may the LORD your God be with you!" 2 CHRONICLES 36:23 NLT

What does that mean to me?

God can get anyone—even one's so-called enemies—to do His work.

Philadelphia

Where is Philadelphia?

In today's western Turkey.

What's it all about?

In the Bible book of Revelation, Jesus had some words for seven churches, Philadelphia being one of them. Because its members were great followers, He said others would know "that you are the ones I love" (Revelation 3:9 NLT).

What's an important verse about Philadelphia?

"Write this letter to the angel of the church in Philadelphia. . . . I know all the things you do, and I have opened a door for you that no one can close. You have little strength, yet you obeyed my word and did not deny me." REVELATION 3:7–8 NLT

What does that mean to me?

Are you following God as much as your strength allows? If so, look for doors He is opening for you!

Philippi

Where is Philippi?

In today's country of Greece.

What's it all about?

Lydia lived in Philippi. She invited the apostle Paul to start a church in her home, which became the first church in Europe.

What's an important verse about Philippi?

We traveled to Philippi, a Roman colony. . . . One of those listening was a woman named Lydia. She was from the city of Thyatira. Her business was selling purple cloth. She was a worshiper of God. The Lord opened her heart to accept Paul's message. ACTS 16:12, 14

What does that mean to me?

Your job is to tell people about God's love. It's His job to open their hearts to receive the wonders of it.

Red Sea

Where is the Red Sea?

Between the continents of Africa and Arabia.

What's it all about?

After Egypt went through ten plagues, its pharaoh finally agreed to free the Jewish slaves. But then he changed his mind. Pharaoh and his army chased after the Israelites, following them into the Red Sea—where he and his army drowned.

What's an important verse about the Red Sea?

Then Moses reached his hand out over the Red Sea. All that night the LORD pushed the sea back with a strong east wind. He turned the sea into dry land. The waters were parted. EXODUS 14:21–22

What does that mean to me?

If God is powerful enough to push back the sea, He's powerful enough to rescue you from anything and anyone.

Rome

Where is Rome?

In Italy.

What's it all about?

The apostle Paul was arrested during a riot in Jerusalem. Then he had to travel to Rome to be tried in a court there. While in prison in Rome, Paul ended up telling many people about God.

What are some important verses about Rome?

That night the Lord appeared to Paul and said, "Be encouraged, Paul. Just as you have been a witness to me here in Jerusalem, you must preach the Good News in Rome as well." ACTS 23:11 NLT

For the next two years, Paul lived in Rome at his own expense. He welcomed all who visited him, boldly proclaiming the Kingdom of God and teaching about the Lord Jesus Christ. And no one tried to stop him. ACTS 28:30–31 NLT

What does that mean to me?

God has a plan for your life, so don't worry about what's happening—or not happening. And don't worry about where you are, because God will always put you right where He needs you.

Samaria

Where is Samaria?

In Israel.

What's it all about?

In Jesus' day, Jews hated people from Samaria. That's why His Jewish listeners didn't like His story about how two of their worship leaders walked right by an injured man lying on the road. Even worse, it was a dreaded Samaritan who *did* help the man and proved himself a wonderful neighbor.

What's an important verse about Samaria?

"Going over to him, the Samaritan soothed his wounds with olive oil and wine and bandaged them. Then he put the man on his own donkey and took him to an inn, where he took care of him." LUKE 10:34 NLT

What does that mean to me?

Being a good neighbor means showing kindness to everyone—no matter who they (or you) are!

Sardis

Where is Sardis?

In today's country of Turkey.

What's it all about?

In Revelation, the last book of the Bible, Jesus had some words for seven churches—Sardis was one of them.

What's an important verse about Sardis?

"Here is what I command you to write to the church in Sardis. . . . 'Remember what you have been taught and have heard. Obey it. Turn away from your sins.'"
REVELATION 3:1, 3

What does that mean to me?

To be a true follower of Jesus, you must not just read His Word (the Bible) but also do what it says. Then you will win over evil—and be good with God!

Sea of Galilee

Where is the Sea of Galilee?

In Israel.

What's it all about?

The Sea of Galilee is really a lake. Here Jesus first met some of His fishermen disciples and walked on water.

What are some important verses about the Sea of Galilee?

Jesus made the disciples get into the boat. He had them go on ahead of him to the other side of the Sea of Galilee. . . . Peter got out of the boat. He walked on the water toward Jesus. But when Peter saw the wind, he was afraid. He began to sink. MATTHEW 14:22, 29–30

One day Jesus said to his disciples, "Let's cross to the other side of the lake." . . . When Jesus woke up, he rebuked the wind and the raging waves. Suddenly the storm stopped and all was calm. LUKE 8:22, 24 NLT

What does that mean to me?

With your eyes on Jesus, you can do anything. And with Him in your boat, you need not fear any storms!

Shiloh

Where is Shiloh?

North of Jerusalem, Israel.

What's it all about?

Shiloh was where Joshua divided up the Promised Land and set up the tent of the tabernacle of God. Later in Shiloh, Hannah prayed for a son from God—and got one. Later the Philistines stole the Ark from Shiloh and the town was destroyed.

What are some important verses about Shiloh?

Once after a sacrificial meal at Shiloh, Hannah got up and went to pray [for a son]. . . . When the child was weaned, Hannah took him to the Tabernacle in Shiloh. . . . The LORD continued to appear at Shiloh and gave messages to Samuel there. 1 SAMUEL 1:9, 24; 3:21 NLT

"Go now to the place at Shiloh where I once put the Tabernacle that bore my name. See what I did there because of all the wickedness of my people, the Israelites. . . . I destroyed Shiloh."
JEREMIAH 7:12, 14 NLT

What does that mean to me?

God lifts up the good and brings down the evil.

Shunem

In Israel, south of Nazareth.

What's it all about?

A wealthy woman in Shunem was nice to God's prophet Elisha. In return for her kindness, he promised God would give her a son. And God did! Later, when that son died, Elisha brought him back to life.

What's an important verse about Shunem?

One day Elisha went to the town of Shunem. A wealthy woman lived there, and she urged him to come to her home for a meal. After that, whenever he passed that way, he would stop there for something to eat.
2 KINGS 4:8 NLT

What does that mean to me?

When you are kind to God's people, God shines His favor on you!

Siloam Pool

Where is the Siloam Pool?

Inside the walls of Jerusalem, Israel.

What's it all about?

King Hezekiah's workers built a tunnel from the spring outside Jerusalem's walls to what was named the Siloam Pool, which was right inside the city walls. Hundreds of years later, Jesus sent a blind man to that pool to wash his eyes.

What's an important verse about the Siloam Pool?

[Jesus] spit on the ground. He made some mud with the spit. Then he put the mud on the man's eyes. "Go," he told him. "Wash in the Pool of Siloam." Siloam means Sent. So the man went and washed. And he came home able to see. JOHN 9:6–7

What does that mean to me?

If you have a problem, go to Jesus. He'll open your eyes.

Smyrna

Where is Smyrna?

In today's country of Turkey.

What's it all about?

In Revelation, the last book of the Bible, Jesus had some words for seven churches—Smyrna was one of them. He had nothing but good things to say about members of that church! Because they were great followers who suffered, He promised them eternal life.

What's an important verse about Smyrna?

"Here is what I command you to write to the church in Smyrna. . . . 'I know that you suffer and are poor. But you are rich!'" REVELATION 2:8–9

What does that mean to me?

Having Jesus in your life is better than anything on earth—even gold! He is your true treasure.

Sodom

Where is Sodom?

Either near or under the Dead Sea.

What's it all about?

Along with its sister city of Gomorrah, Sodom was full of people who behaved very badly. Because Abraham asked God to spare any godly people in the cities, the Lord sent angels to rescue Abraham's nephew Lot.

What's an important verse about Sodom?

[Abraham] looked down toward Sodom and Gomorrah and the whole valley. . . . When God destroyed the cities of the valley, he showed concern for Abraham. He brought Lot out safely when he destroyed the cities where Lot had lived. GENESIS 19:28–29

What does that mean to me?

God listens to your prayers and rescues those you love. Who can you pray for today?

Sychar

Where is Sychar?

In Samaria.

What's it all about?

Jesus stopped to rest at a well in Sychar. There He met a woman. He told her many things about herself—and that her spirit would never thirst with Him, the living water, in her life. After their talk, she went and told others that He must be the Christ, the one who would save them all.

What's an important verse about Sychar?

Many of the Samaritans from the town of Sychar believed in Jesus. They believed because of the woman's witness. She said, "He told me everything I've ever done." JOHN 4:39

What does that mean to me?

Jesus knows everything about you. So trust Him with your life—and drink in His never-ending love!

Tarshish

Where is Tarshish?

Somewhere west of Israel.

What's it all about?

God told Jonah to tell the evil people in Nineveh that God was going to destroy their town. But Jonah didn't obey Him. Jonah went the other way and ended up in the belly of a huge fish. Later he *did* go to Nineveh after all.

What's an important verse about Tarshish?

Jonah. . .went down to Joppa and found a ship which was going to Tarshish. Jonah paid money, and got on the ship to go with them, to get away from the Lord.
JONAH 1:3 NLV

What does that mean to me?

No matter where you go, God will always find a way to turn you back around to doing what *He* thinks is best.

Thessalonica

Where is Thessalonica?

In today's country of Greece.

What's it all about?

Paul and his friends went to Thessalonica to tell its people about Jesus. The Thessalonians joyfully followed the example of these Christian workers.

What's an important verse about Thessalonica?

We are sending this letter to you, the members of the church in Thessalonica. . . . You welcomed our message with the joy the Holy Spirit gives. So you became a model to all the believers in the lands of Macedonia and Achaia.
1 THESSALONIANS 1:1, 6–7

What does that mean to me?

Do your best to be like Jesus. And before you know it, others will be following your example.

Thyatira

Where is Thyatira?

In today's country of Turkey.

What's it all about?

In Revelation, the last book of the Bible, Jesus had some words for seven churches—Thyatira was one of them. Even though some of its people were remaining faithful to Jesus, some were listening to Jezebel, an evil teacher in their church.

What's an important verse about Thyatira?

"Write this to the angel of the church in the city of Thyatira. . . . 'You are allowing Jezebel who calls herself a preacher to teach my servants. She is leading them in the wrong way.'" REVELATION 2:18, 20 NLV

What does that mean to me?

To stay on the right track, follow the words of Jesus. He will teach you all the right ways to live.

Troas

Where is Troas?

In today's country of Turkey.

What's it all about?

In Troas, Paul was preaching late into the night. As Paul talked and talked, the young man Eutychus was sitting on a windowsill. He ended up not only falling asleep but falling out the window!

What's an important verse about Troas?

[Eutychus] fell sound asleep and dropped three stories to his death below. Paul went down, bent over him, and took him into his arms. "Don't worry," he said, "he's alive!" . . . Meanwhile, the young man was taken home alive and well, and everyone was greatly relieved.
ACTS 20:9–10, 12 NLT

What does that mean to me?

Make sure you keep your ears—and eyes—wide open to the Word of God!

Ur

Where is Ur?

In today's country of Iraq.

What's it all about?

Abraham was born and brought up in Ur and later moved to Haran. Then God told him to go to a land God would show him. And the faithful Abraham left.

What's an important verse about Ur?

"You are the LORD God, who chose Abram and brought him from Ur of the Chaldeans and renamed him Abraham. When he had proved himself faithful, you made a covenant with him. . . . And you have done what you promised, for you are always true to your word."
NEHEMIAH 9:7–8 NLT

What does that mean to me?

God always keeps His promises—no matter where you go or where He sends you.

Uz

Where is Uz?

Somewhere in the Middle East—no one knows for sure.

What's it all about?

Job, a man of God, was rich in faith, family, animals, wealth, and health. First the devil took his stuff—including his family. Then he attacked Job's body. But because Job never cursed God, he gained more in the end than he had in the beginning of his story.

What's an important verse about Uz?

There was a man who lived in the land of Uz. His name was Job. He was honest. He did what was right. He had respect for God and avoided evil. JOB 1:1

What does that mean to me?

When, no matter what, you stick things out with God, you will be even more blessed!

Zarephath

Where is Zarephath?

In today's country of Lebanon.

What's it all about?

God sent Elijah to a widow in Zarephath for food. But she had no bread—only a little flour and oil. So Elijah told her to make some bread with what little she did have, and God would make sure she had enough.

What's an important verse about Zarephath?

Elijah had food every day. There was also food for the woman and her family. The jar of flour wasn't used up. The jug always had oil in it. That's what the LORD had said would happen. 1 KINGS 17:15–16

What does that mean to me?

God has a way of making a lot out of a little—so use what you have for Him, and you'll have more than enough.

Introduction

The Bible is a fascinating book. Although it contains hundreds of stories from Genesis to Revelation, it is really one continuous tale revealing not only God's unending love for His people—you and me—but the idea that God has made us unique for a reason! We are each here to play a part in His amazing plan.

Starring in the Bible's many stories are more than 3,000 different people. In this book, we have chosen 99 of the most interesting and important people—both men and women—of scripture. Every sketch follows this outline:

- *Who is this person?*
- *When did he/she live?*
- *What's his/her story?*
- *What's an important verse about him/her?*
- *So what?*

One of the great things about the Bible is the fact that we can learn so much from those who have gone before. We can see ourselves in each story—even though it may have happened thousands of years before we were even born.

Use this fun, fact-filled book to better understand yesterday, guide yourself today, and discover God's plan for your future.

Aaron

Who is Aaron?

Older brother of Moses; Israel's first "high priest."

About 3,500 years ago.

What's his story?

One word: Mouth

In more words: God's people, the Israelites, were slaves in Egypt. So God told Moses to go see Egypt's king—or pharaoh—and tell him to free God's people. But Moses had trouble talking. So his brother, Aaron, spoke for him, telling the pharaoh to let God's people go.

Aaron also

- made a golden calf;
- did miracles with his staff;
- wore special robes.

What's an important verse about him?

[The Lord] said, "Is not Aaron the Levite your brother? I know he can speak well. . . . He will be a mouth for you." EXODUS 4:14, 16 NLV

So what?

When Aaron let others talk him into things that were against God—like making a golden calf for the people to worship instead of God—he got into trouble. But when Aaron listened to God, miracles happened. If you follow God, He'll use you in a mighty way.

Abigail

Who is Abigail?

Widow of Nabal; wife of King David.

When did she live?

About 3,000 years ago.

What's her story?

One word: Sensible

In more words: Nabal wouldn't feed King David and his men even though they'd guarded Nabal's sheep. So David planned to attack Nabal. But Abigail got some food and rode out to meet David and his army before anyone was harmed.

What's an important verse about her?

[David told Abigail,] "The LORD. . .has sent you today to find me. . . . You have shown a lot of good sense. You have kept me from killing Nabal and his men this very day."
1 SAMUEL 25:32–33

So what?

God is willing to give you good sense to do the right thing in every situation. All you have to do is ask Him.

Abraham

Who is Abraham?

The Father of Many Nations; also called Abram; husband of Sarah.

When did he live?

About 4,000 years ago.

What's his story?

One word: Faith

In more words: When Abraham was seventy-five years old, God told him to leave his home in Haran. So Abraham got up and left. He did whatever God told him to do—even sacrificing his own son, who was saved by God at the last minute!

Abraham also

- had two sons, Ishmael and Isaac;
- was very rich;
- believed God's promises.

What's an important verse about him?

Abraham had faith. So he obeyed God. God called him to go to a place he would later receive as his own. So he went. He did it even though he didn't know where he was going. HEBREWS 11:8

So what?

Like Abraham, you, too, can step out in faith. When you do, good things happen!

Adam

Who is Adam?

The first man; husband of Eve.

When did he live?

Day 6 of Creation, thousands of years ago.

What's his story?

One word: First

In more words: God created Adam to look just like Him. Then He planted Adam and Eve in the Garden of Eden. God warned them not to eat from a certain tree—but they did anyway. Then they hid from God. But God found them, clothed them, and then kicked them out of Eden.

Adam also

- named all the animals;
- was the father of Abel, Cain, and Seth;
- brought sin into the world by disobeying God.

What's an important verse about him?

And the LORD God made clothing from animal skins for Adam and his wife. GENESIS 3:21 NLT

So what?

Whether you are first or last, good or bad, hiding or seeking, God will take care of you.

Andrew

Who is Andrew?

Fisherman; brother of Simon Peter; disciple of Jesus.

When did he live?

About 2,000 years ago.

What's his story?

One word: Fisherman

In more words: Andrew was a follower of John the Baptist. When John pointed out Jesus as the Lamb of God, Andrew then followed Jesus. Andrew brought many people to Jesus, including his brother Simon Peter and the boy with five loaves and two fish.

What's an important verse about him?

Peter and his brother Andrew. . .were throwing a net into the lake. They were fishermen. "Come. Follow me," Jesus said. "I will make you fishers of people."
MATTHEW 4:18–19

So what?

When you get how great Jesus is, you can't help but follow Him only and bring others to Him.

Anna

Who is Anna?

A prophet.

When did she live?

About 2,000 years ago.

What's her story?

One word: Worshipper

In more words: Anna was a very old widow. She worshipped God at the Jewish temple—all day and all night. She even went without food so that she could pray better. When baby Jesus' parents brought Him to the temple, Anna praised God because she knew the child would save God's people.

What's an important verse about her?

She talked about the child to everyone who had been waiting expectantly for God to rescue Jerusalem. LUKE 2:38 NLT

So what?

Like Anna, if you spend lots of time with God, worshipping and praying, you will know when His promises come true.

Balaam

Who is Balaam?

A magician.

When did he live?

About 3,400 years ago.

What's his story?

One word: Untrustworthy

In more words: One day a king convinced Balaam to curse the Israelites. But a talking donkey opened up Balaam's eyes—and ears—to God's will and way. So Balaam ended up blessing, instead of cursing, God's people. Later, Balaam turned away from God again.

What's an important verse about him?

The Ammonites and Moabites had hired Balaam to call a curse down on them. But our God turned the curse into a blessing. NEHEMIAH 13:2

So what?

Don't worry if something not so good happens. God has a way of changing what seems to be bad into something really good. You can trust God!

Barnabas

Who is Barnabas?

An early Christian.

When did he live?

About 2,000 years ago.

What's his story?

One word: Encourager

In more words: One of the early church leaders was named Joseph. He was such a cheerleader for Christianity, he was nicknamed Barnabas, which means "Son of Encouragement." Because Barnabas had such a good heart, lots of people began following Jesus.

What's an important verse about him?

When [Barnabas] arrived and saw this evidence of God's blessing, he was filled with joy, and he encouraged the believers to stay true to the Lord. ACTS 11:23 NLT

So what?

When we help and cheer on others, we draw them closer and closer to Jesus. Who can you encourage today?

Bartimaeus

Who is Bartimaeus?

A blind beggar.

When did he live?

About 2,000 years ago.

What's his story?

One word: Determined

In more words: Bartimaeus was a blind beggar sitting by the road in Jericho. When he heard Jesus was near, he began to yell for Jesus to heal him. Others told Bartimaeus to be quiet, but he was too determined. Finally, Jesus called him over and healed him! Then he followed Jesus.

What's an important verse about him?

"Be quiet!" many of the people yelled at him. But [Bartimaeus] only shouted louder, "Son of David, have mercy on me!" MARK 10:48 NLT

So what?

When it comes to faith and prayer, be persistent. Don't let anyone—or anything—stop you from talking to and believing in Jesus!

Bathsheba

Who is Bathsheba?

Widow of Uriah; wife of King David;
mom to King Solomon; ancestor of Jesus.

When did she live?

About 3,000 years ago.

What's her story?

One word: Coveted

In more words: David wanted Uriah's wife, Bathsheba.
So he slept with her. She got pregnant. So David murdered
her husband and made Bathsheba his queen. But trouble
followed, beginning with the death of their first child.

What's an important verse about her?

David. . .was walking on the roof of the palace. As he
looked out over the city, he noticed a woman of unusual
beauty taking a bath. 2 SAMUEL 11:2 NLT

So what?

God says, "You must not covet" (Deuteronomy 5:21 NLT).
That's because when you want (covet) something that
belongs to someone else, trouble follows. So play it safe—
stay on your own roof and don't take a bath outside.

Boaz

Husband of Ruth; ancestor of King David and Jesus.

When did he live?

About 3,200 years ago.

What's his story?

One word: Kind

In more words: Boaz was a rich relative of Ruth's dead husband. When Ruth, a foreigner, came to Israel with her mother-in-law, Naomi, Boaz was very kind to Ruth—so kind that he married her! They had a son, Obed.

What's an important verse about him?

[Ruth said to Boaz,] "You have comforted me. You have spoken kindly to me. And I'm not even as important as one of your female servants!" Ruth 2:13

So what?

Boaz's kindness won the hearts of his servants, relatives, and friends. God rewarded him by making him the great-grandfather of a king! Who can you bless with kindness today?

Caiaphas

Who is Caiaphas?

Jewish high priest in Jesus' day.

When did he live?

About 2,000 years ago.

What's his story?

One word: Know-it-all

In more words: After Jesus raised Lazarus from the dead, Caiaphas worried he would lose his power. So he talked other leaders into having Jesus arrested, tried, and crucified. Little did Caiaphas know that what he did was part of God's master plan.

What's an important about him?

Caiaphas, who was high priest at that time, said, "You don't know what you're talking about! You don't realize that it's better for you that one man should die for the people." JOHN 11:49–50 NLT

So what?

No matter what anyone does—good or evil—God will use it for His own ends. He is the only true know-it-all.

Cornelius

Who is Cornelius?

An Italian army captain from Caesarea.

When did he live?

About 2,000 years ago.

What's his story?

One word: Giver

In more words: Cornelius prayed to the Jews' God and gave lots of gifts to others. An angel told him to invite Simon Peter to his house. When Peter got there, he preached and the Holy Spirit came. Then Cornelius, his family, and his servants were baptized as Christians.

What's an important verse about him?

Jewish followers who had come along with Peter were surprised and wondered because the gift of the Holy Spirit was also given to the people who were not Jews.
ACTS 10:45 NLV

So what?

When you give gifts to God and others, He can't help but give gifts back—to anyone who will take them!

Damaris

A Greek woman.

When did she live?

About 2,000 years ago.

What's her story?

One word: Convert

In more words: The apostle Paul preached a really good sermon in Athens, Greece, on a rocky hill named after the Roman god of war—Mars. After Paul's speech, Damaris believed in Christ. She converted (or turned) from following many gods to following the one true God.

What's an important verse about her?

Some people followed him and became Christians. One was Dionysius, a leader in the city. A woman named Damaris believed. And there were others also. ACTS 17:34 NLV

So what?

God can use any of us to bring somebody to Christ. Will you let Him use you?

Daniel

Who is Daniel?

Boy brought from Judah to serve foreign kings.

When did he live?

About 2,500 years ago.

What's his story?

One word: Tamer

In more words: King Darius made a law that everyone had to pray to him. But Daniel would only pray to the one true God, and he did so three times a day. So Daniel was thrown into the lions' den for disobeying Darius. But because Daniel was faithful, God saved him!

Daniel also

- was named Belteshazzar;
- told a king the meaning of his dreams;
- saw the fingers of a human hand write on a wall.

What's an important verse about him?

[Daniel told King Darius,] "My God sent his angel. And his angel shut the mouths of the lions. They haven't hurt me at all. That's because I haven't done anything wrong in God's sight." DANIEL 6:22

So what?

When you make much prayer a habit, God can use you in a mighty way. He may even give you the power to tame beasts!

David

Who is David?

King of Israel; father of King Solomon; ancestor of Jesus.

When did he live?

About 3,000 years ago.

What's his story?

One word: Praiser

In more words: God chose David to be the second king of Israel. And even though David made lots of mistakes—slept with a married woman, murdered her husband, disobeyed God—he was still the apple of God's eye. Why? Because he gave his full heart to God.

David also

- killed the giant Goliath;
- led a team of 30 mighty men;
- wrote many psalms praising God.

What's an important verse about him?

"God removed Saul and replaced him with David, a man about whom God said, 'I have found David son of Jesse, a man after my own heart. He will do everything I want him to do.'" ACTS 13:22 NLT

So what?

Want to be the apple of God's eye and a giant slayer? Then do everything God asks you to do!

Deborah

Who is Deborah the prophetess?

Prophet and judge of Israel; wife of Lappidoth.

About 3,300 years ago.

What's her story?

One word: Willing

In more words: The Israelites were being attacked by King Jabin of Canaan. God told Deborah that the Israelites could beat Jabin's 900 iron chariots. But Barak, her army commander, would not lead the men into battle unless Deborah went along. She did, and the Israelites won!

Deborah also

- is the only woman judge of Israel in the Bible;
- usually settled fights while sitting under a palm tree;
- kept the peace in the land for 40 years.

What's an important verse about her?

There were few people left in the villages of Israel—until Deborah arose as a mother for Israel. JUDGES 5:7 NLT

So what?

When God called on Deborah, she answered, always willing to do whatever He asked. What is God asking you to do? Are you willing?

Delilah

Who is Delilah?

Dangerous Philistine woman.

When did she live?

About 3,300 years ago.

What's her story?

One word: Greedy

In more words: Samson fell in love with Delilah. Some Philistines, enemies of the Jews, said they would pay her silver coins if she could learn the secret of Samson's strength. She nagged Samson until he finally told her; his strength was in his hair.

What's an important verse about her?

She called in a man to shave off the seven locks of his hair. In this way she began to bring him down, and his strength left him. JUDGES 16:19 NLT

So what?

Greedy people can be dangerous. Beware of those who love silver and gold more than God and other people.

Dorcas

Who is Dorcas?

Christian from Joppa;
also called Tabitha.

When did she live?

About 2,000 years ago.

What's her story?

One word: Do-gooder

In more words: Dorcas was a Christian woman who
helped lots of people. When she got sick and died,
believers sent for Peter. He found Dorcas's body in her
room, weeping widows all around her. A few moments
later, Peter's faith resulted in a miracle!

What's an important verse about her?

Peter asked them all to leave the room; then he knelt and
prayed. Turning to the body he said, "Get up, Tabitha."
And she opened her eyes! ACTS 9:40 NLT

So what?

Dorcas used her gifts to do good works in her hometown.
What God-given gifts are you using to show the Lord's love?

Elijah

Who is Elijah?

Prophet; miracle worker.

When did he live?

About 3,000 years ago.

What's his story?

One word: Pray-er

In more words: Because of his closeness to God, Elijah's prayers made miracles happen. They raised people from the dead, made oil appear, brought fire down from heaven, stopped the Jordan River from flowing, and more!

Elijah also

- was fed by ravens, then heard God whisper;
- went up to heaven in a chariot of fire;
- appeared on a mountain with Moses and Jesus in bright light.

What's an important verse about him?

"LORD my God, give this boy's life back to him!"
The LORD answered Elijah's prayer. He gave the boy's life back to him. So the boy lived. 1 KINGS 17:21–22

So what?

Elijah did many great and special things. But he was only a human whose real power was in prayer and his special relationship with God. You, too, can be an Elijah! Just keep praying to and listening for God.

Elizabeth

Who is Elizabeth?

Zechariah's wife; John the Baptist's mom; Mary's cousin.

When did she live?

About 2,000 years ago.

What's her story?

One word: Faithful

In more words: Elizabeth and her husband, Zechariah, were old and had no children. But they stayed faithful to God. One day, the angel Gabriel announced that Elizabeth would become pregnant. She later gave birth to John the Baptist, the one who would call Jesus the Lamb of God.

What's an important verse about her?

The angel said to him, "Do not be afraid, Zechariah. Your prayer has been heard. Your wife Elizabeth will have a child. It will be a boy, and you must name him John." LUKE 1:13

So what?

God blesses and fulfills the dreams of those who are faithful to Him—during good times and bad.

Enoch

Who is Enoch?

Son of Jared; father of Methuselah.

When did he live?

Thousands of years ago.

What's his story?

One word: Disappeared

In more words: Enoch was the head of the seventh family that came after Adam. Enoch was 65 years old when his own son Methuselah was born. After that, Enoch walked very closely with God for another 300 years on earth. Then one day, Enoch just disappeared.

What's an important verse about him?

Enoch had faith. So he was taken from this life. He didn't die. He just couldn't be found. God had taken him away. Before God took him, Enoch was praised as one who pleased God. HEBREWS 11:5

So what?

Amazing things happen when you walk very closely with God.

Esther

Who is Esther?

Orphan girl; King Xerxes' wife and queen.

When did she live?

About 2,500 years ago.

What's her story?

One word: Risk-taker

In more words: Haman, King Xerxes' top man, decided to rid the kingdom of all Jews. When Queen Esther's cousin Mordecai found out about it, he sent a message to Esther to go before the king to save the Israelites. She did so—even though it might have meant her death.

Esther also
- was a beautiful woman;
- had lots of courage;
- cared more about others than herself.

What's an important verse about her?

"Who knows if perhaps you were made queen for just such a time as this?" ESTHER 4:14 NLT

So what?

God needs all kinds of people to serve Him at all different times and in all different ways. Ask God how He can use you at such a time as this.

Eve

First woman; wife of Adam.

When did she live?

Day 6 of Creation, thousands of years ago.

What's her story?

One word: Pushover

In more words: God created Eve, a partner for Adam in the Garden of Eden. God told them both not to eat a certain fruit. But a serpent (Satan) easily talked Eve into disobeying God by eating the lovely-looking fruit and offering it to Adam. As a result, sin entered our world.

What's an important verse about her?

The man called his wife's name Eve, because she was the mother of all living. GENESIS 3:20 NLV

So what?

Eve is the mother of us all. Sometimes, like her, we are easily talked into disobeying God. When you feel tempted, ask God for help. Don't be a pushover for evil.

Ezekiel

Who is Ezekiel?

Prophet and priest.

When did he live?

About 2,600 years ago.

What's his story?

One word: Messenger

In more words: Ezekiel was given many dreams from God. Visions of flying four-faced angels, battling skeletons, and more contained special messages that Ezekiel was to give God's people. These were dark days when Israel was destroyed and her people taken away from their homes.

What's an important verse about him?

"Son of man, I have chosen you to be a watchman over the people of Israel. Whenever you hear a word from My mouth, tell them of the danger." EZEKIEL 3:17 NLV

So what?

Even during hard times, God has a good message for believers. Look for it in your Bible.

Ezra

Who is Ezra?

Writer.

When did he live?

About 2,500 years ago.

What's his story?

One word: Student

In more words: While Ezra was being held captive in Babylon, he studied the Law of Moses. When the king let him go to Jerusalem, Ezra read God's Law to everyone. He also taught the Jews how to apply it to their lives. Because of Ezra, many people turned back to God.

What's an important verse about him?

Ezra had set his heart to learn the Law of the Lord, to live by it, and to teach His Laws in Israel. EZRA 7:10 NLV

So what?

To get a good start in life, be like Ezra—a student of God's Word. Then use what you learn to obey God and help others!

Gideon

Who is Gideon?

Son of Joash; soldier for Israel.

When did he live?

About 3,350 years ago.

What's his story?

One word: Overcomer

In more words: When called by God to battle his enemy, Gideon thought he was too feeble. But God knew what Gideon was made of—strength, not weakness. The first thing the angel of God said to Gideon was, "Mighty warrior, the LORD is with you" (Judges 6:12).

What's an important verse about him?

Gideon asked, "How can I possibly save Israel? My family group is the weakest in the tribe of Manasseh. And I'm the least important member of my family." JUDGES 6:15

So what?

Believe that God has already given you all the strength you need to serve Him!

Goliath

Who is Goliath?

Giant Philistine warrior.

When did he live?

About 3,000 years ago.

What's his story?

One word: Darer

In more words: Goliath was huge—more than nine feet tall! And every day on the battlefield, he would dare someone from Israel to fight him. David the shepherd boy took up Goliath's challenge. He shut the giant's mouth, killing him with a sling and one rock!

What's an important verse about him?

David said to Goliath, "You are coming to fight against me with a sword, a spear and a javelin. But I'm coming against you in the name of the LORD who rules over all." 1 SAMUEL 17:45

So what?

Your giant-slaying power is the presence of the Lord with and within you.

Hagar

Who is Hagar?

Slave; mother of Ishmael.

When did she live?

About 4,200 years ago.

What's her story?

One word: Slave

In more words: Hagar was Sarah's slave. She was given to Abraham so that he could have a son—Ishmael. Later Sarah had a son by Abraham—Isaac. Then Sarah had Abraham send Hagar and Ishmael away. The two almost died from lack of water in the desert.

What's an important verse about her?

God opened Hagar's eyes. And she saw a well of water. She went and filled the leather bag with water and gave the boy a drink. GENESIS 21:19 NLV

So what?

No matter how bad things may seem, God can open your eyes so that you can find whatever you need.

Hannah

Wife of Elkanah; mother of Samuel.

When did she live?

About 4,100 years ago.

What's her story?

One word: Wholehearted

In more words: Elkanah had two wives—Peninnah, who had children; and Hannah, who did not. Even though Hannah had Elkanah's love, she very much wanted babies. So with all her heart and soul, she cried and prayed to God, who answered her. She gave birth to a baby boy—and then many more!

Hannah also
- named her son Samuel, which means "God hears";
- gave her firstborn son back to God;
- sang a song of thanks to God.

What's an important verse about her?

"I was pouring out my soul to the Lord. . . . For I have been speaking out of much trouble and pain in my spirit."
1 SAMUEL 1:15–16 NLV

So what?

Pray to God with your whole heart. He will hear and answer you again and again.

Herod the Great

Who is Herod the Great?

Part-Jewish, part-Roman king of Judea.

When did he live?

About 2,000 years ago.

What's his story?

One word: Jealous

In more words: Rome called Herod "King of the Jews." When wise men came to Jerusalem, looking for a just-born king of the Jews, Herod got jealous—so jealous that he had all boys two years old and younger killed. But God had other plans for that just-born king named Jesus.

What's an important verse about him?

An angel of the Lord came to Joseph in a dream. He said, "Get up. Take the young Child and His mother to the country of Egypt. . . . Herod is going to look for the young Child to kill Him." MATTHEW 2:13 NLV

So what?

You can be sure that nothing can stop God and His plans for you—and me!

Isaac

Who is Isaac?

Son of Abraham and Sarah; husband of Rebekah; father of Jacob and Esau.

When did he live?

About 4,100 years ago.

What's his story?

One word: Promised

In more words: God promised Abraham that he would be the father of many nations, beginning with the birth of a son in Abraham and Sarah's old age. God kept His promise! When Abraham was 100 and Sarah 90, Isaac was born—and later saved from being sacrificed.

What's an important verse about him?

The Lord visited Sarah as He had said and did for her as He had promised. Sarah. . .gave birth to a son.
GENESIS 21:1–2 NLV

So what?

God always keeps His promises. Find them in your Bible and claim them all!

Isaiah

Who is Isaiah?

Prophet; preacher; author of the Bible book Isaiah.

When did he live?

About 2,800 years ago.

What's his story?

One word: Volunteer

In more words: When God wondered whom He could send to speak to His people, Isaiah answered, "Here I am. Send me!" Isaiah later made lots of prophecies about what would happen in the future—and many came true, even those that described Jesus 800 years before He was born!

What's an important verse about him?

Paul said, "The Holy Spirit spoke the truth to your early fathers through the early preacher Isaiah."
ACTS 28:25 NLV

So what?

Like Isaiah and Jesus, you are part of God's plan. When God calls you, will you say, "Here I am. Send me"?

Jacob

Who is Jacob?

Son of Isaac and Rebekah; twin brother of Esau.

When did he live?

About 4,000 years ago.

What's his story?

One word: Trickster

In more words: Jacob tricked Esau into giving up his rights as the firstborn son. Later, Jacob was often tricked by others. One night, after not letting go of God during a struggle, Jacob was renamed Israel, which means "wrestled with God."

Jacob also

- saw angels going up and down a ladder to heaven;
- got tricked into marrying Leah;
- was father of the twelve tribes of Israel.

What's an important verse about him?

[God told Jacob,] "I am with you, and I will protect you wherever you go. One day I will bring you back to this land. I will not leave you until I have finished giving you everything I have promised you." GENESIS 28:15 NLT

So what?

Do you have a good hold on God? If so, never let Him go—He just can't wait to bless you.

Jael

Wife of Heber the Kenite.

When did she live?

About 3,300 years ago.

What's her story?

One word: Fearless

In more words: The Israelites' commander, Barak, would not face the Canaanites unless Deborah, an Israelite judge, went with him. So Deborah told him God would hand the enemy's commander, Sisera, over to a woman. That woman was Jael, Heber's wife, who lived in a tent.

What's an important verse about her?

Jael picked up a tent stake and a hammer. She went quietly over to Sisera. . .lying there, fast asleep. He was very tired. She drove the stake through his head right into the ground. So he died. JUDGES 4:21

So what?

God uses ordinary people—like you—to do extraordinary things, all according to His plan.

James, Son of Zebedee

Who is James, son of Zebedee?

Fisherman; brother of John; disciple of Jesus.

When did he live?

About 2,000 years ago.

What's his story?

One word: Martyr

In more words: Disciple James, along with his brother John and their friend Peter, was especially close to Jesus. All three were with Jesus when He was transfigured and when He was praying in the garden. James was the first follower killed (or martyred) for being a Christian.

What's an important verse about him?

King Herod. . .had James killed with a sword.
ACTS 12:1–2

So what?

Do you, like James, love Jesus more than life itself?

Jeremiah

Who is Jeremiah?

Weeping prophet; writer of the Bible book Jeremiah.

When did he live?

About 2,600 years ago.

What's his story?

One word: Go-getter

In more words: Once he answered God's call, Jeremiah was held in a dungeon, put in a muddy pit, whipped, attacked, and imprisoned. But he never gave up giving people God's messages and hoping they would turn back to the Lord.

What's an important verse about him?

"Before I started to put you together in your mother, I knew you. Before you were born. . . . I chose you to speak to the nations for Me." JEREMIAH 1:5 NLV

So what?

Imagine—God has known you forever! He knows why you were made and will help you do what He calls you to do.

Jesus

Who is Jesus?

Son of God; son of Mary; son of foster father, Joseph; the Messiah, the Christ.

When did He live?

About 2,000 years ago.

What's His story?

One word: Savior

In more words: After the angel Gabriel spoke to a woman named Mary, the Holy Spirit visited her and she got pregnant. She and her husband, Joseph, then traveled to Bethlehem. There, Jesus was born in a stable. Shepherds and wise men bearing gifts came to visit this special child. When He grew up, He told many stories that taught people how to live good lives.

Jesus also

- raised people from the dead;
- cured the sick, lame, deaf, dumb, and blind;
- stopped the wind and waves;
- died on the cross to save us from sin, guilt, and death;
- rose from the dead;
- became the bridge between us and God.

What's an important verse about Him?

In the beginning, the Word was already there. The Word was with God, and the Word was God. . . . All things were made through him. . . . The Word became a human being. He made his home with us. JOHN 1:1, 3, 14

Then Jesus got up and ordered the winds and the waves to stop. It became completely calm. The disciples were amazed. They asked, "What kind of man is this? Even the winds and the waves obey him!" MATTHEW 8:26–27

So what?

Jesus, the Word, has been around since the very beginning. He came to earth to save us. When you open up your heart to Him, He lives in you.

When Jesus speaks, amazing things happen. What is He saying to you today? If you're not sure, check out your Bible. What verses really touch you? That's Jesus speaking. Listen, learn, and obey.

Jezebel

Who is Jezebel?

Wife of King Ahab of Israel.

When did she live?

About 2,900 years ago.

What's her story?

One word: Wicked

In more words: Jezebel worshipped a god called
Baal and a goddess called Asherah. Jezebel wanted the
people of Israel to do the same. She killed a lot of Jewish
prophets. Jezebel talked Ahab into doing many wicked
things, too. And she tried to have Elijah killed.

What's an important verse about her?

"The Lord, the God of Israel, says. . . 'The dogs will eat
Jezebel in the land of Jezreel. No one will bury her.' "
2 KINGS 9:6, 10 NLV

So what?

Wicked ways lead to wicked ends. Stay close to God, do
good, and all will be well.

Joanna

Who is Joanna?

Wife of Cuza.

When did she live?

About 2,000 years ago.

What's her story?

One word: Provider

In more words: Joanna, who had been healed by Jesus, became one of His followers. Because she was married to Cuza, the man who ran King Herod's household, she had enough money to buy supplies for Jesus and His twelve disciples.

What's an important verse about her?

It was Mary Magdalene, Joanna, Mary the mother of James, and several other women who told the apostles what had happened. LUKE 24:10 NLT

So what?

Joanna saw the angels in Jesus' tomb! When you follow Jesus closely, you, too, will see amazing things happen. But don't forget to tell others!

Job

Who is Job?

Rich man of the East.

When did he live?

No one knows for sure. Maybe 4,000 years ago!

What's his story?

One word: Patient

In more words: Job was a very good man with lots of animals, land, and children. One day, God let Satan test Job. So Satan had all of Job's things and children taken away from him. He even gave Job boils on his skin. But Job kept trusting God.

Job also

- was married to a woman who told him to curse God and die;
- had a long conversation with God Himself!
- ended up with more at the end than he had at the beginning.

What's an important verse about him?

People who don't give up are blessed. You have heard that Job was patient. And you have seen what the Lord finally did for him. JAMES 5:11

So what?

No matter how good you may be, bad things can still happen. But be patient. Stick with God, and everything will turn out all right in the end!

Jochebed

Who is Jochebed?

Wife of Amram; mother of Moses, Aaron, and Miriam.

When did she live?

About 3,500 years ago.

What's her story?

One word: Clever

In more words: When Moses was born, the Egyptian king ordered that all the Hebrew boy babies be killed. So Jochebed saved her baby, Moses, by putting him in a basket and hiding him in the river. There the king's daughter saw him and raised him as her own.

What's an important verse about her?

"Take this baby and nurse him for me," the princess told the baby's mother. "I will pay you for your help." So the woman took her baby home and nursed him. EXODUS 2:9 NLT

So what?

When you use your brain and, more importantly, trust God, He will reward you!

John the Apostle

Who is John the Apostle?

Brother of James; son of Salome and Zebedee; disciple of Jesus; writer.

When did he live?

About 2,000 years ago.

What's his story?

One word: Loved

In more words: John the Apostle wrote the book of John in the Bible. There he calls himself "the disciple Jesus loved." John also wrote 1 John, 2 John, 3 John, and Revelation. While Jesus was on the cross, He told John to take care of Mary, Jesus' mother. And he did.

What's an important verse about him?

Dear children, let's not merely say that we love each other; let us show the truth by our actions. 1 JOHN 3:18 NLT

So what?

Jesus loves you very much. Will you, like John, show Jesus' love to someone else today?

John the Baptist

Who is John the Baptist?

Son of Zechariah and Elizabeth; cousin of Jesus.

When did he live?

About 2,000 years ago.

What's his story?

One word: Pointer

In more words: The angel Gabriel told Zechariah that he and his wife would have a child in their old age. That child was John the Baptist. He wore weird clothes and ate locusts. But when he saw Jesus, he knew He was the Son of God. And John pointed everyone to Him!

John the Baptist also

- baptized lots of people;
- saw the Holy Spirit land on Jesus, like a dove;
- was beheaded by Herod Antipas.

What's an important verse about him?

[John said,] "I am filled with joy at [Jesus'] success. He must become greater and greater, and I must become less and less." JOHN 3:29–30 NLT

So what?

To be a true follower of Jesus, we must make knowing Jesus more important than anything we do well or right. For what can you praise Jesus—instead of yourself—today?

Jonah

Who is Jonah?

Prophet.

When did he live?

About 2,700 years ago.

What's his story?

One word: Runaway

In more words: God told Jonah to go to Nineveh to talk to people there. But Jonah was afraid, so he jumped on a ship going the other way. After he was thrown overboard, a sea creature swallowed Jonah. After Jonah prayed to God, the creature spit him out on land, and Jonah went to Nineveh.

What's an important verse about him?

Now the LORD had arranged for a great fish to swallow Jonah. And Jonah was inside the fish for three days and three nights. JONAH 1:17 NLT

So what?

When God asks you to do something, it's better to obey than run away. What has God been asking you to do?

Jonathan

Who is Jonathan?

Son of King Saul.

When did he live?

About 3,000 years ago.

What's his story?

One word: Friend

In more words: Jonathan was a good leader of his father's army and also David's best friend. When King Saul wanted to kill David, Jonathan risked his own life and his dad's anger to save David. Later, Jonathan died on the battlefield as he fought for his father.

What's an important verse about him?

The soul of Jonathan became one with the soul of David. Jonathan loved him as himself. 1 SAMUEL 18:1 NLV

So what?

Look for a good friend who shares your faith in God. That will be a friendship you will always treasure, one that will gladden your heart.

Joseph of Arimathea

Who is Joseph of Arimathea?

Member of the Jewish Council.

When did he live?

About 2,000 years ago.

What's his story?

One word: Bold

In more words: When the Jewish leaders decided that Jesus should be put to death, Councilman Joseph of Arimathea did not agree. That's because he was a follower of Jesus. But he had kept this a secret because he feared what the Jews might do to him.

What's an important verse about him?

Joseph went boldly to Pilate and asked for Jesus' body. . . . He put it in a tomb cut out of rock. MARK 15:43, 46

So what?

At first you might be afraid of someone or something. But in the end, God will give you the courage to do what's right.

Joseph, Foster Father of Jesus

Who is Joseph

Carpenter; husband of Mary.

When did he live?

About 2,000 years ago.

What's his story?

One word: Guided

In more words: Four times an angel of the Lord talked to Joseph in a dream. First, an angel told him to marry the already-pregnant Mary. Second, to keep baby Jesus safe, the angel told Joseph to take Jesus to Egypt. Third, the angel told him to go back to Israel, and the fourth message was to head to Galilee.

What's an important verse about him?

Joseph awoke from his sleep. He did what the angel of the Lord told him to do. MATTHEW 1:24 NLV

So what?

Once you start to follow God's orders, He will continue to guide you—over and over again.

Joseph, Son of Jacob

Who is Joseph, son of Jacob?

Shepherd, slave, prisoner, ruler.

When did he live?

About 4,000 years ago.

What's his story?

One word: Dreamer

In more words: Joseph dreamed he would rule over his father and brothers someday. After he told his family about his dream, his brothers sold him to traveling salesmen. So Joseph went from shepherd to slave to prisoner—but ended up a ruler in Egypt.

Joseph also

- wore a really colorful coat;
- told people what their dreams meant;
- never lost hope in God.

What's an important verse about him?

"You planned to do a bad thing to me. But God planned it for good, to make it happen that many people should be kept alive, as they are today." GENESIS 50:20 NLV

So what?

If things don't go as planned, don't give up or get upset. Just do the next thing! Keep hoping in God. He will turn whatever seems bad into something that will get you one step closer to your dreams!

Joshua

Who is Joshua?

Moses' assistant; Israel's next leader.

When did he live?

About 3,400 years ago.

What's his story?

One word: Loyal

In more words: When Moses sent men out to look over the Promised Land, only Caleb and Joshua said that the Israelites could defeat the giants in that land. Joshua led many battles, including the one at Jericho. When Moses died, Joshua became the Jews' next leader.

Joshua also

- led God's people into the Promised Land;
- always obeyed God;
- defeated 31 kings.

What's an important verse about him?

"Choose today whom you will serve. . . . As for me and my family, we will serve the LORD." JOSHUA 24:15 NLT

So what?

Joshua is a good example of what happens when we serve God—and God alone. When you stick to God, you can be sure He will stick to you!

Josiah

Who is Josiah?

Sixteenth king of Judah.

When did he live?

About 2,600 years ago.

What's his story?

One word: Focused

    In more words: When he was eight, Josiah became king and had the temple fixed up. There, a book of Moses' Law was found. The good and great King Josiah had it read to him. Then he read it to his people.

What's an important verse about him?

There was no king like Josiah. . . . He followed the LORD with all his heart and all his soul. . .with all his strength. He did everything the Law of Moses required.
2 KINGS 23:25

So what?

When your eyes and heart are on God's Word, He will lead you—to be the best you can be!

Judas Iscariot

Who is Judas Iscariot?

Disciple of Jesus.

When did he live?

About 2,000 years ago.

What's his story?

One word: Traitor

In more words: Keeper of the disciples' money bag, Judas often stole coins for himself. He was later paid thirty silver pieces for leading temple guards to Gethsemane. There Judas kissed Jesus so the soldiers would know whom to arrest. Afterward, Judas felt bad for what he'd done.

What's an important verse about him?

"I have sinned," he said. "I handed over a man who is not guilty." . . . Judas threw the money into the temple and left. Then he went away and hanged himself.
MATTHEW 27:4–5

So what?

To truly follow Jesus, love God and others more than money and yourself!

Lazarus

Who is Lazarus?

Brother of Mary and Martha.

When did he live?

About 2,000 years ago.

What's his story?

One word: Glory

In more words: Lazarus, Jesus' friend, was sick. His sisters sent a message to Jesus. But Jesus stayed where He was. By the time Jesus got to His friend, Lazarus had been dead for four days. It didn't matter. Jesus raised him from the dead! And many then believed!

What's an important verse about him?

Jesus. . .said, "Lazarus's sickness will not end in death. No, it happened for the glory of God so that the Son of God will receive glory from this." JOHN 11:4 NLT

So what?

Never moan. God can make something good come out of anything!

Leah

Who is Leah?

First wife of Jacob; sister of Rachel.

When did she live?

About 4,000 years ago.

What's her story?

One word: Unloved

In more words: One night Jacob was to marry the woman he loved—Rachel, Laban's younger daughter. But Laban sent Leah into the dark tent instead of Rachel, thus tricking Jacob into marrying the older sister. An ancestor of Jesus, Leah gave Jacob six sons.

What's an important verse about her?

The LORD saw that Jacob didn't love Leah as much as he loved Rachel. So he let Leah have children. But Rachel wasn't able to. GENESIS 29:31

So what?

Even if, like Leah, you feel unloved, just keep your faith in God. He will bless and love you all the more!

Lot

Who is Lot?

Abraham's nephew.

When did he live?

About 4,000 years ago.

What's his story?

One word: Drifter

In more words: Lot and Abraham had so many animals, there wasn't enough land for the men to stay together. So Lot chose to go live near the evil city of Sodom. The farther from Abraham he got, the further he drifted into trouble. But because Lot kept trusting God, angels rescued him.

What's an important verse about him?

God saved Lot. He was a man who did what was right. He was shocked by the dirty, sinful lives of people who didn't obey God's laws. 2 PETER 2:7

So what?

Even if trouble is all around you, don't be afraid. Trust God. He'll save you!

Luke

Who is Luke?

Doctor; missionary; writer; follower of Jesus.

When did he live?

About 2,000 years ago.

What's his story?

One word: Reporter

In more words: Luke wrote the Bible book called Luke. There he gives all the facts of Jesus' life and the miracles He did. Luke also wrote the Bible book of Acts, in which he tells of mission trips he had with the apostle Paul.

What's an important verse about him?

I have looked with care into these things from the beginning. I have decided it would be good to write them to you one after the other the way they happened. Then you can be sure you know the truth about the things you have been taught. LUKE 1:3–4 NLV

So what?

You, too, can be a fact-seeker. Take time each day to read God's truth in the Bible!

Lydia

Who is Lydia?

Seller of cloth; first European Christian.

When did she live

About 2,000 years ago.

What's her story?

One word: Open

In more words: Lydia was a woman who sold expensive purple cloth. Seeing her and other women sitting on a riverbank at a prayer meeting, Paul sat down and spoke to them. Lydia believed what Paul was saying. So she and her whole house were baptized!

What's an important verse about her?

As [Lydia] listened to us, the Lord opened her heart, and she accepted what Paul was saying. ACTS 16:14 NLT

So what?

Next time you hear or read God's Word, be like Lydia. Open up your ears—and your heart!

Mark

Who is Mark?

Gospel writer; also called John Mark.

When did he live?

About 2,000 years ago.

What's his story?

One word: Runner

In more words: When Jesus was arrested, one young man, probably Mark, ran away so fast he left his clothes behind! Mark also went on a mission trip with Paul and Barnabas, only to run off in the middle of it. Mark made some mistakes, but in the end, he helped Paul and others.

What's an important verse about him?

[The apostle Paul wrote:] Only Luke is with me. Get Mark and bring him with you. He helps me in my work for the Lord. 2 TIMOTHY 4:11

So what?

It's okay if you make mistakes—as long as you learn and grow from them.

Martha

Who is Martha?

Sister of Mary and Lazarus.

When did she live?

About 2,000 years ago.

What's her story?

One word: Busy

In more words: When Jesus was at Martha's house, her sister, Mary, sat at Jesus' feet, listening to Him. That made Martha mad. So Martha whined to Jesus. She wanted Him to tell Mary to help her make dinner!

What's an important verse about her?

"Martha, Martha," the Lord answered. "You are worried and upset about many things. But only one thing is needed. Mary has chosen what is better. And it will not be taken away from her." LUKE 10:41–42

So what?

You probably have lots to do. But spending time with Jesus is the best thing to do!

Mary Magdalene

Who is Mary Magdalene?

Follower of Jesus.

When did she live?

About 2,000 years ago.

What's her story?

One word: Free

In more words: Jesus chased seven demons out of Mary Magdalene. Because of that, she was a very thankful follower. She gave money to support Jesus and His disciples. Mary was one of the few with Jesus when He died on the cross. She was the first to see Him after His death.

Mary Magdalene also

- brought burial spices to anoint Jesus' body;
- saw the stone rolled away from Jesus' tomb;
- spoke to two angels.

What's an important verse about her?

Mary Magdalene found the disciples and told them, "I have seen the Lord!" Then she gave them his message.
JOHN 20:18 NLT

So what?

Jesus has freed you from sin. Have you told anyone about Him today?

Mary of Bethany

Who is Mary of Bethany?

Sister of Martha and Lazarus.

When did she live?

About 2,000 years ago.

What's her story?

One word: Remembered

In more words: Mary of Bethany wanted to spend time being with and listening to Jesus. She did that rather than preparing dinner for her guests. She left that work to her sister, Martha. Her loyalty to Jesus will never be forgotten.

What's an important verse about her?

"She has poured this perfume on me to prepare my body for burial. I tell you the truth, wherever the Good News is preached throughout the world, this woman's deed will be remembered and discussed." MATTHEW 26:12–13 NLT

So what?

Spend lots of time hanging with Jesus and you, too, will be remembered!

Mary, Mother of Jesus

Who is Mary, mother of Jesus?

Mother of God's Son; wife of Joseph.

When did she live?

About 2,000 years ago.

What's her story?

One word: Wonderer

In more words: The angel Gabriel came and told Mary she would be the mother of God's Son. And she was. After she gave birth to Jesus, angels spoke to shepherds, telling them where they could find Christ the Lord. When they visited Jesus and told their story, Mary wondered about their words.

Mary also

- was an ordinary woman yet an extraordinary servant of God;
- saw Jesus change water into wine;
- was with Jesus at His death.

What's an important verse about her?

Mary said, "I am willing to be used of the Lord. Let it happen to me as you have said." Then the angel went away from her. LUKE 1:38 NLV

So what?

Mary was willing to be used by God—mind, body, and spirit. Because of that, amazing things happened in her life. Are you a willing servant of God?

Matthew

Who is Matthew?

Follower of Jesus; writer; also called Levi.

When did he live?

About 2,000 years ago.

What's his story?

One word: Tracker

In more words: Matthew collected and kept track of taxes. When he left everything to follow Jesus, God used Matthew's talents in a new way. Matthew kept track of Jesus' doings on earth and wrote them out for us—in the Bible book of Matthew!

What's an important verse about him?

He walked farther and saw Levi (Matthew). . .sitting at his work gathering taxes. Jesus said to him, "Follow Me." Levi got up and followed Him. MARK 2:14 NLV

So what?

Are you following Jesus? If so, how is God using you in a new way?

Melchizedek

Who is Melchizedek?

King of Salem; priest of God Most High.

When did he live?

About 4,000 years ago.

What's his story?

One word: Mysterious

In more words: Melchizedek met Abraham one day. He reminded Abraham to give God the praise for a victory in battle. Then Melchizedek disappeared from scripture. Some people think this Old Testament priest was actually Jesus.

What's an important verse about him?

Melchizedek has no father or mother. He has no family line. His days have no beginning. His life has no end. He remains a priest forever, just like the Son of God. HEBREWS 7:3

So what?

When things go well, do you praise God? After all, it's no mystery that it's His doing, right?

Methuselah

Who is Methuselah?

Son of Enoch.

When did he live?

Thousands of years ago.

What's his story?

One word: Ancient

In more words: Methuselah is the oldest of the old! He is the longest-living human being recorded in the Bible. He was 187 years old when he became the father of Lamech. Although Methuselah's father, Enoch, went up with God, Methuselah did eventually pass away—but only after having other sons and daughters.

What's an important verse about him?

Methuselah lived 969 years, and he died.
GENESIS 5:27 NLV

So what?

God decides how long you will live. But only you can decide what you will do while you're here. Will you use your time to help God and love others?

Miriam

Who is Miriam?

Sister of Aaron and Moses.

When did she live?

About 3,500 years ago.

What's her story?

One word: Green-eyed

In more words: Miriam was a good sister to Moses—until she and Aaron tried to bring him down. Because of her green-eyed jealousy of Moses, God gave Miriam leprosy, a skin-eating disease. Moses, a good brother, asked God to heal his sister. And God did.

What's an important verse about her?

Miriam and Aaron spoke against Moses. . . . "Is it true that the Lord has spoken only through Moses? Has He not spoken through us also?" NUMBERS 12:1–2 NLV

So what?

Take care not to raise yourself up by bringing down someone you envy. That kind of jealousy will only eat away at you.

Mordecai

Who is Mordecai?

Relative of Esther.

When did he live?

About 2,500 years ago.

What's his story?

One word: Refuser

In more words: Haman, one of King Xerxes' officials, was mad. Whenever he walked by, Mordecai refused to bow. Mordecai would worship no one but God. So Haman made plans to have Mordecai and all other Jews killed. Later, it turned out Haman had to bow to Mordecai—and Haman was killed.

What's an important verse about him?

Mordecai the Jew. . .found favor in the eyes of his people. He worked for the good of his people and spoke for the well-being of all the Jews. ESTHER 10:3 NLV

So what?

When you worship only God—and not people—
only good will come of it.

Moses

Who is Moses?

Son of Jochebed and Amram; brother of Aaron and Miriam; husband of Zipporah; writer of first five Old Testament books.

When did he live?

About 3,500 years ago.

What's his story?

One word: Self-doubting

In more words: Out of a burning bush, God spoke to Moses. God said He would be sending Moses to Pharaoh, asking him to let God's people out of Egypt. But Moses doubted he could do all God wanted. God disagreed. He had already prepared Moses to do the deeds—and Moses did.

Moses also

- was raised by Pharaoh's daughter;
- killed an Egyptian who was beating a Jewish slave;
- ran away and became a shepherd;
- parted the Red Sea;
- received God's Law on two stone tablets;
- led the Israelites to the Promised Land.

What's an important verse about him?

Moses protested to God, "Who am I to appear before Pharaoh? Who am I to lead the people of Israel out of Egypt?" God answered, "I will be with you."
EXODUS 3:11–12 NLT

Since then, Israel has never had a prophet like Moses. The LORD knew him face to face. Moses did many miraculous signs and wonders. The LORD had sent him to do them in Egypt. DEUTERONOMY 34:10–11

So what?

No matter who you are, you can do what God calls you to do—because He is with you!

If you trust God, He will give you the power to do amazing things! Seek His face today and find out what He wants you to do.

Naaman

Who is Naaman?

Army commander.

When did he live?

About 2,900 years ago.

What's his story?

One word: Prideful

In more words: Naaman was an army hero with leprosy, a skin disease. His wife's servant girl told him a prophet of Israel, Elisha, could heal him. When Naaman went to see the prophet, Elisha didn't come out but sent a message to wash in the Jordan seven times. That hurt Naaman's pride.

What's an important verse about him?

Naaman went away angry. He said, "I was sure he would come out to me." 2 KINGS 5:11

So what?

Once Naaman swallowed his pride, he went down to the river, washed, and was healed. He teaches you to not let pride stand in the way of God's work in your life.

Naomi

Who is Naomi?

Wife of Elimelech; mother-in-law of Ruth.

When did she live?

About 3,200 years ago.

What's her story?

One word: Hopeful

In more words: Naomi and her family moved from
Israel to Moab during a drought. There, Naomi's husband
and sons died. She was very sad. So she decided to go
back to Israel. Ruth, her daughter-in-law, went with her.
There, Naomi became a grandmother.

What's an important verse about her?

Naomi said to her daughter-in-law. . . . "The LORD is still
being kind to those who are living and those who are
dead." RUTH 2:20

So what?

No matter how bad things look, keep hoping. God will
not fail you.

Nathan

Prophet.

When did he live?

About 3,000 years ago.

What's his story?

One word: Adviser

In more words: King David wanted to build a temple for the Lord. But God told Nathan to tell David that Solomon was to build God's house. David was very disappointed. Then God, speaking through Nathan, told David that the Lord had other plans—like David's son (Jesus) taking over another kind of throne.

What's an important verse about him?

"I will never take my love away from your son. I will place him over my house and my kingdom forever. His throne will last forever." 1 CHRONICLES 17:13–14

So what?

God puts wise people in our lives to help us. Who can you ask for advice?

Nebuchadnezzar

Who is Nebuchadnezzar?

King of Babylon.

When did he live?

About 2,600 years ago.

What's his story?

One word: Braggart

In more words: One day while walking on his palace roof, King Nebuchadnezzar bragged about his great deeds, power, and palace. That's when God told Nebuchadnezzar he would change into a beast. Later, when Nebuchadnezzar came to his senses, he became a king again.

What's an important verse about him?

My body became wet with the dew of heaven. I stayed that way until my hair grew like the feathers of an eagle. My nails became like the claws of a bird. DANIEL 4:33

So what?

Beastly pride can turn you into an animal. Stay humble and human by thanking God for all you've got.

Nehemiah

Who is Nehemiah?

Prophet; king's wine taster.

When did he live?

About 2,500 years ago.

What's his story?

One word: Builder

In more words: Nehemiah heard about Jerusalem's broken-down wall. Its gates had been burned. This made him sad. The king told Nehemiah he could leave Iran and go fix Jerusalem's wall. Because of his great faith in God, Nehemiah and the people rebuilt the wall in only fifty-two days!

What's an important verse about him?

"The God of heaven will help us succeed. We, his servants, will start rebuilding this wall." NEHEMIAH 2:20 NLT

So what?

Put all your trust in God and put your hand to the task He gives you. Then He will make what seems undoable doable!

Nicodemus

Who is Nicodemus?

Jewish council member and Pharisee.

When did he live?

About 2,000 years ago.

What's his story?

One word: Learner

In more words: Nicodemus was a well-thought-of Jewish teacher. He went to talk to Jesus at night, when others wouldn't see him. Nicodemus asked Jesus several questions, which Jesus answered. After dying on the cross, Jesus was buried by Joseph of Arimathea and Nicodemus.

What's an important verse about him?

Jesus replied, "You are a respected Jewish teacher, and yet you don't understand these things?" JOHN 3:10 NLT

So what?

If you have a question, go to Jesus and His Word. People willing to learn are always growing closer to God—in heaven and on earth.

Noah

Who is Noah?

Ark builder.

When did he live?

Thousands of years ago.

What's his story?

One word: Boatman

In more words: People on earth were behaving badly. So God decided to start over with good Noah and his family. God told him to build an ark and fill it with animals, two by two. Then Noah's family got on the boat to be safe from the flood that came with forty days and nights of rain.

Noah also

- built the ark in 120 years;
- had three sons;
- lived 950 years.

What's an important verse about him?

God. . .brought the flood on the world of sinners. But Noah was a preacher of right living. He and his family of seven were the only ones God saved.
2 PETER 2:5 NLV

So what?

If you do right by God, He will do right by you.

Paul

Who is Paul?

Pharisee known as Saul; killer of Christians;
preacher to Christians; tentmaker and writer.

When did he live?

About 2,000 years ago.

What's his story?

One word: Missionary

In more words: Saul mistreated many Christians. Then, while he was on the road, he saw a flash of light and fell to the ground. He heard Jesus speak from heaven, asking why Saul was against Him. When Saul's friends led him away, he was blind. Later, Saul was healed and believed in Jesus Christ. Once Saul, now Paul, he traveled the world, spreading the Good News.

Paul also
- gave the okay to stone Stephen;
- took three missionary journeys;
- spent lots of time in prisons;
- wrote many letters to churches;
- was shipwrecked on the island of Malta;
- lived after getting bitten by a poisonous snake.

What's an important verse about him?

I focus on this one thing: Forgetting the past and looking forward to what lies ahead, I press on to reach the end of the race and receive the heavenly prize for which God, through Christ Jesus, is calling us. PHILIPPIANS 3:13–14 NLT

So what?

Don't worry about what happened yesterday. Focus on winning with Jesus today!

Peter

Who is Peter?

Fisherman; brother of Andrew; disciple of Jesus; also called Simon Peter.

When did he live?

About 2,000 years ago.

What's his story?

One word: Rock

In more words: Peter was one of three disciples closest to Jesus. But Jesus told Peter that three times he would deny knowing Jesus, and then a rooster would crow. And that's just what happened after Jesus was arrested. Three times a frightened Peter told people that he didn't know Jesus. Then Peter heard "Cock-a-doodle-doo!"

Peter also

- healed many people;
- spent time in prison;
- wrote the Bible books of 1 and 2 Peter.

What's an important verse about him?

"And I tell you that you are Peter. On this rock I will build My church. The powers of hell will not be able to have power over My church." MATTHEW 16:18 NLV

So what?

Jesus can use you for great things—even if you make mistakes.

Philemon

Who is Philemon?

Friend of Paul; "owner" of Onesimus.

When did he live?

About 2,000 years ago.

What's his story?

One word: Master

In more words: Onesimus, Philemon's slave, had run away from Philemon and met up with Paul in prison. Onesimus became a Christian. In his letter, Paul tells Philemon he is sending Onesimus back and hopes Philemon will treat the man as a brother, not as a slave.

What's an important verse about him?

Any favor you do must be done because you want to do it, not because you have to. PHILEMON 1:14

So what?

God loves people who truly want to help brothers and sisters. What are you willing to do for others—and God—today?

Pontius Pilate

Who is Pontius Pilate?

Roman governor of Judea.

When did he live?

About 2,000 years ago.

What's his story?

One word: Appeaser

In more words: Pilate was an appeaser. That means he often gave in to what others wanted, even though he knew he was right! Pilate knew Jesus had committed no crime. But because the crowd demanded Jesus' death, Pilate caved.

What's an important verse about him?

Pilate wanted to satisfy the crowd. So he. . .ordered that Jesus be whipped. Then he handed him over to be nailed to a cross. MARK 15:15

So what?

Ask God for help when you are making decisions. He'll help you to do the right thing—even if it doesn't please someone else.

Priscilla

Who is Priscilla?

Wife of Aquila; tentmaker.

When did she live?

About 2,000 years ago.

What's her story?

One word: Coworker

In more words: Priscilla was a busy woman. She was not only a housewife and tentmaker, but she also traveled and worked with Paul, studied the Good News about Jesus, taught many people about Christ, held church services at her house—and more!

What's an important verse about her?

Priscilla and Aquila. . .almost died for me. I am thankful for them. All the churches that were started among the people who are not Jews are thankful for them also.
Romans 16:3–4 NLV

So what?

When you work for Christ, there's no telling how much you will change the world for the good!

Rachel

Who is Rachel?

Wife of Jacob; mother of Joseph and Benjamin.

When did she live?

About 4,000 years ago.

What's her story?

One word: Dissatisfied

In more words: Rachel was very beautiful. Jacob truly loved her, not her sister, Leah. But neither of those things made Rachel happy. She demanded children from Jacob. But then, when she gave birth to her son Joseph, instead of being satisfied with one, she said, "May the Lord give me another son."

What's an important verse about her?

When Rachel saw that she had not given birth to any children for Jacob, she became jealous of her sister. She said to Jacob, "Give me children, or else I am going to die!" GENESIS 30:1 NLV

So what?

If you are satisfied and thankful for all that God has given you, He will give you more.

Rahab

Body seller; ancestor of David and Jesus.

When did she live?

About 3,400 years ago.

What's her story?

One word: Spared

In more words: Rahab was a woman who sold to men the use of her body. When Joshua sent spies to check out Jericho, Rahab saved (or spared) them from being killed. That's because she had heard what their God had done and believed in His power.

What's an important verse about her?

Rahab, the prostitute, had faith. So she welcomed the spies. That's why she wasn't killed with those who didn't obey God. HEBREWS 11:31

So what?

God can use anyone. All you have to do is have faith and courage. Then He will do great things through you!

Rebekah

Who is Rebekah?

Isaac's wife; Esau and Jacob's mom.

When did she live?

About 4,100 years ago.

What's her story?

One word: Willful

In more words: Rebekah had twin boys—Esau and Jacob. She liked Jacob the best. But her husband, Isaac, liked Esau. When it was time for the older son, Esau, to get his father's blessing, Rebekah came up with a plan for Jacob to get the blessing instead. This made for problems later.

What's an important verse about her?

Esau hated Jacob because their father had given Jacob the blessing. And Esau began to scheme: "I will soon be mourning my father's death. Then I will kill my brother, Jacob." GENESIS 27:41 NLT

So what?

Things work out better when you follow God's will rather than your own.

Rhoda

Who is Rhoda?

Servant girl.

When did she live?

About 2,000 years ago.

What's her story?

One word: Overjoyed!

In more words: Rhoda worked at the house of Mary, the mother of John Mark. Many Christians were there one night. They were praying Peter would be freed from prison. And he was! An angel got him out. Afterward Peter went right to Mary's house and knocked on the door.

What's an important verse about her?

Rhoda came to open it. When she recognized Peter's voice, she was so overjoyed that, instead of opening the door, she ran back inside and told everyone, "Peter is standing at the door!" ACTS 12:13–14 NLT

So what?

When God answers your prayers, let everyone see your joy!

Ruth

Who is Ruth?

Moabite daughter-in-law of Naomi; widow of Mahlon; wife of Boaz; mother of Obed.

When did she live?

About 3,200 years ago.

What's her story?

One word: Loyal

In more words: Naomi's husband and two married sons died, leaving her all alone. So Naomi left Moab to go back to Israel. Ruth, now a widow herself, went along, not wanting to leave her mother-in-law. In Israel, Ruth worked in Boaz's fields. Then he married her.

What's an important verse about her?

"I will go where you go. I will live where you live. Your people will be my people. And your God will be my God."
RUTH 1:16–17 NLV

So what?

God loves it when His people are loyal to each other—and Him.

Samson

Who is Samson?

Judge of Israel; son of Manoah.

About 3,300 years ago.

What's his story?

One word: Strongman

In more words: Samson was born to an old couple who had been visited by an angel. He was to be a Nazirite—set apart for God's use. But he broke the Nazirite rules. When Delilah cut his hair, Samson lost his strength. The Philistines gouged his eyes out and put him in prison.

Samson also

- killed a lion with his bare hands;
- killed 1,000 Philistines with the jawbone of a donkey;
- killed more Philistines at his death than he did in life.

What's an important verse about him?

Samson called to the Lord and said, "O Lord God, I beg You. Remember me. Give me strength only this once, O God. So I may now punish the Philistines for my two eyes." Judges 16:28 NLV

So what?

Even if you make mistakes, God can still use you—from the beginning of your life to the end.

Samuel

Who is Samuel?

Judge, prophet, priest of Israel; son of Elkanah and Hannah.

When did he live?

About 4,100 years ago.

What's his story?

One word: Listener

In more words: Samuel (which means "heard of God") was born in answer to his mother, Hannah's, prayer for a son. As a boy, he served Eli the priest. Later, Samuel put oil on the heads of Israel's first two kings, announcing them as picked by God.

What's an important verse about him?

Then the Lord came and stood and called as He did the other times, "Samuel! Samuel!" And Samuel said, "Speak, for Your servant is listening." 1 SAMUEL 3:10 NLV

So what?

Tell God you're listening. Then wait for Him to speak.

Sapphira

Ananias's wife.

About 2,000 years ago.

One word: Liar

    In more words: Some Christians were selling their land and possessions, then giving the money to the church. Ananias and Sapphira sold some land—but Peter knew Ananias kept part of the money for himself. When he brought money to Peter, Ananias dropped dead.

Peter said to her, "How could you two have talked together about lying to the Holy Spirit? See! Those who buried your husband are standing at the door and they will carry you out also." At once she fell down at his feet and died.
ACTS 5:9–10 NLV

You can't hide anything from God. So be honest about everything to everyone—including Him.

371

Sarah

Who is Sarah?

Wife of Abraham; mother of Isaac.

When did she live?

About 4,000 years ago.

What's her story?

One word: Laughter

In more words: One day God visited Abraham. He told him that Abraham's wife, Sarah, would give birth to a son in one year. By then, Abraham would be 100 years old and Sarah would be 90. So she started laughing because she couldn't believe what God was promising! But you know what? Their son, Isaac, was born one year later!

What's an important verse about her?

"Is anything too hard for the Lord?"
GENESIS 18:14 NLV

So what?

Don't laugh off what seems undoable. Your God can do anything! That's what makes Him God!

Saul, King of Israel

Who is Saul, king of Israel?

First king God chose to rule Israel.

When did he live?

About 3,000 years ago.

What's his story?

One word: Rebel

In more words: Saul appeared to be handsome, brave, and obedient. But he made some pretty bad choices. Several times he disobeyed God. So God decided to replace Saul with David—someone who really loved and obeyed God from the heart.

What's an important verse about him?

"You haven't obeyed the command the LORD your God gave you. . . . Now your kingdom won't last."
1 SAMUEL 13:13–14

So what?

God wants you to obey Him—with all your mind and your heart and your soul.

Shiphrah

Who is Shiphrah?

Jewish midwife.

When did she live?

About 3,500 years ago.

What's her story?

One word: Daring

In more words: Shiphrah and Puah were Hebrews who helped other women give birth in Egypt. The king of Egypt told them to kill all the Jewish boy babies because there were so many Hebrews. Because Shiphrah and Puah loved God, they dared to disobey the king. They let the Hebrew baby boys live.

What's an important verse about her?

So God was good to the midwives, and the Israelites continued to multiply, growing more and more powerful. And because the midwives feared God, he gave them families of their own. EXODUS 1:20–21 NLT

So what?

God will reward you for your courage and obedience to Him.

Solomon

Who is Solomon?

King of Israel; son of David and Bathsheba; writer of Song of Solomon, Ecclesiastes, and many psalms and proverbs.

When did he live?

About 3,000 years ago.

What's his story?

One word: Wise

In more words: When Solomon became king, he didn't ask God for a long life, riches, or fame. Instead, Solomon asked for wisdom to rule. God was so pleased He gave the king not only wisdom but riches and honor as well. But when Solomon stopped looking to God for answers, trouble began.

Solomon also
- built God's temple;
- built his own palace;
- had a throne of ivory.

What's an important verse about him?

Trust in the LORD with all your heart;
  do not depend on your own understanding.
Seek his will in all you do,
  and he will show you which path to take.
PROVERBS 3:5–6 NLT

So what?

Need wisdom? Don't rely on your smarts. Go to God and His Word. He has lots of wisdom to share!

Stephen

Who is Stephen?

Faithful Christian; martyr.

When did he live?

About 2,000 years ago.

What's his story?

One word: Christlike

In more words: Stephen had lots of faith. He also was full of the Holy Spirit. He performed lots of miracles and preached to Jewish leaders. They got so mad that they dragged him out of the city and threw stones at him. Saul (later Paul) was a witness to this.

What's an important verse about him?

As they stoned him, Stephen prayed, "Lord Jesus, receive my spirit." He fell to his knees, shouting, "Lord, don't charge them with this sin!" And with that, he died.
ACTS 7:59–60 NLT

So what?

To be like Christ, we must love all others—no matter what they do.

Thomas

Who is Thomas?

Disciple of Jesus; nicknamed the Twin.

When did he live?

About 2,000 years ago.

What's his story?

One word: Doubter

In more words: When Jesus rose from the grave, He appeared to all the disciples—except Thomas. When Thomas's other friends told him they'd seen the Lord, Thomas doubted them! One week later, Jesus appeared again to the disciples. Thomas was there—then he believed!

What's an important verse about him?

Jesus told him, "You believe because you have seen me. Blessed are those who believe without seeing me." JOHN 20:29 NLT

So what?

Even though you haven't seen Jesus, you believe in Him. You are blessed because you have taken His Word as proof that He is real!

Timothy

Who is Timothy?

Missionary; pastor; friend of Paul the apostle.

When did he live?

About 2,000 years ago.

What's his story?

One word: Timid

In more words: Timothy was half Greek and half Jewish. When he met Paul, he became a Christian. He traveled with Paul on missionary journeys. Then he became a pastor at the church in Ephesus. Paul, who loved Timothy like a son, wrote him two letters, which are in the Bible.

What's an important verse about him?

God did not give us a spirit of fear. He gave us a spirit of power and of love and of a good mind. 2 TIMOTHY 1:7 NLV

So what?

Even if you are young and timid, God can give you the power to do great things. Soon you'll be bigger and bolder!

Titus

Who is Titus?

Greek man who became a Christian.

When did he live?

About 2,000 years ago.

What's his story?

One word: Helper

In more words: Titus traveled with Paul. Then Paul left him in charge of some churches. Titus was a very good preacher. When he was working at the church in Crete, Paul sent him a letter, giving him advice. The letter is called "Titus" and is a book in the Bible.

What's an important verse about him?

[Paul wrote:] Titus is my helper. He and I work together among you. 2 CORINTHIANS 8:23

So what?

God, His churches, and His leaders can use many helpers. What can you do to help God and your church today?

Zacchaeus

Who is Zacchaeus?

Tax collector.

When did he live?

About 2,000 years ago.

What's his story?

One word: Cheater

In more words: Zacchaeus was a greedy tax collector who cheated people. When he heard Jesus was coming to town, he wanted to see Him—but he was too short. So he climbed a tree. When Jesus saw Zacchaeus, He knew who he was right away.

What's an important verse about him?

Zacchaeus stood before the Lord and said, "I will give half my wealth to the poor, Lord, and if I have cheated people on their taxes, I will give them back four times as much!"
Luke 19:8 NLT

So what?

Jesus knows exactly who you are and what you've done. He knows that once you glimpse Him, you'll want to change.

Zechariah, Father of John the Baptist

Who is Zechariah, father of John the Baptist?

Husband of Elizabeth; priest at the temple.

When did he live?

About 2,000 years ago.

What's his story?

One word: Speechless

In more words: Zechariah was serving in the temple when the angel Gabriel came. He told Zechariah he would have a son named John. Old Zechariah didn't believe the angel. So Gabriel made it so Zechariah wouldn't be able to talk until the baby boy was born.

What's an important verse about him?

He wrote, "His name is John." Everyone was amazed. Right away Zechariah could speak again. His first words gave praise to God. LUKE 1:63–64

So what?

God can do awesome things through you, things so amazing they leave you speechless—except for praise!

Zipporah

Who is Zipporah?

Wife of Moses; daughter of Jethro.

When did she live?

About 3,500 years ago.

What's her story?

One word: Fixer

In more words: After murdering an Egyptian, Moses ran away to Midian. There he met Zipporah. The Lord was angry because Moses hadn't performed a Jewish ceremony on his son. So Zipporah did it—to save both Moses and their son.

What's an important verse about her?

She touched Moses' feet with the skin she had cut off. "You are a husband who has forced me to spill my son's blood," she said. So the LORD didn't kill Moses.
EXODUS 4:25–26

So what?

It's never too late to fix your mistakes. God is always ready to forgive everything from A to Z.

Know Your
Bible
for Kids
All About Jesus

Introduction

Jesus is a mysterious, captivating, and awesome person. His story is told from the first to the last page of the Bible. He wants you to know who He was, has been, and always will be—the one who gave His life to save yours so that you could be a part of God's amazing plan.

In this fascinating book, *Know Your Bible for Kids—All About Jesus*, we have chosen 100 of the most interesting things about Jesus, the King of kings and Lord of lords. Every illuminating entry follows this outline:

- *Who, where, or what is this person, place, or thing?*
  A brief description of a character, site, or term.

- *What's it all about?*
  Details about the background of this character, site, or term as it relates to Jesus.

- *What's an important verse about that person, place, or thing?*
  A key Bible verse about that character, site, or term.

- *What does that mean to me?*
  What that character, site, or term teaches God's followers about Jesus.

One of the awesome things about Jesus is that He has always been with us, from Genesis to Revelation.

He is our timeless Rock and Refuge. Within this book, you will rediscover Jesus from A to Z, beginning with the description of Him as the "Alpha and Omega" and concluding with His never-ending reign in "Zion," the heavenly Jerusalem.

You'll learn more and more insights into His nature and His immense love for us all as He comes to life on every page. We invite you to use this fun, fascinating, and fact-filled book to better understand God's plan, His provision of the Spirit, His love for His one and only Son, Jesus, and how, in following Him, you'll find the depth and breadth of Christ in your walk and way every day!

Alpha and Omega

What is the Alpha and Omega?

Alpha and *Omega* are Greek words. In English, *Alpha* means "first" and *Omega* means "last."

What's it all about?

A man named John had a revelation or vision. In it, he heard Jesus call Himself "the Alpha and the Omega."

What's an important verse about the Alpha and Omega?

[A voice] said, "(I am the First and the Last.) Write in a book what you see and send it to the seven churches." REVELATION 1:11 NLV

What does that mean to me?

God wants you and everyone else to get His message: Jesus is all powerful. He has been and always will be here, helping you—and everyone else—from the beginning to the end. Jesus is all you will ever need.

Andrew

Who is Andrew?

A fisherman, one of Jesus' main disciples (followers), and a brother of Simon Peter from the town of Bethsaida.

What's it all about?

One day, over 5,000 hungry people came to Jesus. Andrew told Jesus what food they had on hand, but he couldn't see it going very far. Yet after Jesus thanked God for the food, there was enough for everyone—plus leftovers!

What's an important verse about Andrew?

Andrew. . .said, "Here is a boy with five small loaves of barley bread. He also has two small fish. But how far will that go in such a large crowd?" JOHN 6:8–9

What does that mean to me?

Thank God for what you have, and Jesus will grow it into more than you can imagine!

Angels

What are angels?

Heavenly creatures. God sends some out to deliver messages to people. Some guard or take care of people. Others worship God in heaven.

What's it all about?

The angel Gabriel announced the coming of John the Baptist and Jesus. Others warned Jesus' foster father, Joseph, of danger. Angels were with Jesus for His birth, life, death, resurrection (rising from the grave), and ascension (going back to heaven).

What's an important verse about angels?

Are not all the angels spirits who work for God? They are sent out to help those who are to be saved from the punishment of sin. HEBREWS 1:14 NLV

What does that mean to me?

Angels were always looking out for Jesus and His followers, and they are certainly looking out for you, too. Though you may not be able to see them, never fear! Your angels are near!

Ascension

What is the ascension?

When Jesus went up (ascended) to heaven after His resurrection (rising from the dead).

What's it all about?

After ascending to be with Father God, Jesus sent the Holy Spirit to take care of us—just like Jesus promised.

What's an important verse about the ascension?

As they strained to see him rising into heaven, two white-robed men suddenly stood among them. "Men of Galilee," they said. . ."Jesus has been taken from you into heaven, but someday he will return from heaven in the same way you saw him go!" ACTS 1:10–11 NLT

What does that mean to me?

Rest easy. Jesus will be back someday. Meanwhile, the Holy Spirit will guide you and fill you with power!

Author of Faith

Who is the Author of Faith?

Jesus is!

What's it all about?

The life and death of Jesus is an amazing tale that tells us how we can get close to God again. And Jesus is the *author* of that story! By His life, He has shown us how to live right. All we need to do is keep looking to Him for guidance and following the words in His Book. He'll make our way perfect!

What's an important verse about the Author of Faith?

Let us keep on running the race marked out for us. Let us keep looking to Jesus. He is the one who started this journey of faith. And he is the one who completes the journey of faith. . . . So think about him. Then you won't get tired. You won't lose hope. HEBREWS 12:1–3

What does that mean to me?

God has given you everything you need to live a wonderful life with Him. Just keep your eyes and mind on Jesus—and the Author will write you a happy ending!

Baptism

What is baptism?

A Christian ceremony where people who believe in Jesus are dipped in or sprinkled with water.

What's it all about?

John the Baptist baptized lots of people. When he baptized Jesus, heaven opened and God's Spirit, which looked like a dove, landed on Jesus. Then a voice from heaven said, "This is my son who I love." In the early days of the Christian church, believers young and old were baptized.

What's an important verse about baptism?

This baptism has nothing to do with removing dirt from your body. Instead, it promises God that you will keep a clear sense of right and wrong. 1 PETER 3:21

What does that mean to me?

When you are baptized, it symbolizes your faith in God. Your heart is one with the heart of Jesus, and the Holy Spirit will help you understand what is right and wrong in God's eyes.

Barabbas

A murderer who was in prison.

What's it all about?

After being arrested, Jesus was brought to Pilate, a Roman governor. But Pilate found Jesus had done nothing wrong. So he offered to set either Barabbas or Jesus free. The crowd chose Barabbas.

What's an important verse about Barabbas?

"Which one of the two do you want me to let go free?" They said, "Barabbas". . . . Pilate let Barabbas go free but he had men whip Jesus. Then he handed Him over to be nailed to a cross. MATTHEW 27:21, 26 NLV

What does that mean to me?

Jesus died so that even the worst of sinners could be set free. No matter what you have done, Jesus can save you!

Bartimaeus

Who is Bartimaeus?

A blind man sitting along the roadside in Jericho when Jesus walked by.

What's it all about?

Bartimaeus kept yelling for Jesus to have pity on him, even when other people told him to be quiet. When Jesus told His disciples to call the blind man, Bartimaeus took off his coat and ran to Jesus.

What's an important verse about Bartimaeus?

The blind man said to Him, "Lord, I want to see!" Jesus said, "Go! Your faith has healed you." At once he could see and he followed Jesus down the road.
MARK 10:51–52 NLV

What does that mean to me?

Need help? Yell out to Jesus. Then, when He calls you, leave everything behind and run to Him. He'll open your eyes of faith!

Bethany

What is Bethany?

A town about a mile and a half from Jerusalem, Israel.

What's it all about?

Bethany is where Lazarus lived with his sisters, Mary and Martha. It's also where a woman poured expensive perfume on Jesus' feet.

What's an important verse about Bethany?

Jesus led his disciples out to the area near Bethany. Then he lifted up his hands and blessed them. While he was blessing them, he left them. He was taken up into heaven. Then they worshiped him. With great joy, they returned to Jerusalem. LUKE 24:50–52

What does that mean to me?

The love and blessings of Jesus keep coming, even though He is now in heaven. That's news that can make you happy—even on the saddest of days!

Bethlehem

What is Bethlehem?

A town five miles from Jerusalem, Israel. Also called Zion and the City of David, Bethlehem is where Jesus was born.

What's it all about?

Many years ago, God spoke to a prophet named Micah, telling him that someday a ruler would be born in Bethlehem. This ruler would be a shepherd for God's people.

What's an important verse about Bethlehem?

"Today in the town of David a Savior has been born to you. He is the Messiah the Lord. Here is how you will know I am telling you the truth. You will find a baby wrapped in strips of cloth and lying in a manger."
LUKE 2:11–12

What does that mean to me?

You can always trust God. He always keeps His promises. He brought a Savior among us!

Bible

What is the Bible?

A book containing 66 smaller books, each written by prophets inspired by God.

What's it all about?

The Bible has two parts. The first is the Old Testament, which is sometimes called the scriptures or holy book. That has 39 books and was written before Jesus was born. The second part is the New Testament. That has 27 books and was written about Jesus after He ascended to heaven.

What's an important verse about the Bible?

God has breathed life into all Scripture. It is useful for teaching us what is true. It is useful for correcting our mistakes. It is useful for making our lives whole again. It is useful for training us to do what is right. By using Scripture, the servant of God can be completely prepared to do every good thing. 2 TIMOTHY 3:16–17

What does that mean to me?

You can trust the Bible to guide you in all things. You can't go wrong by following what God has written!

Bridegroom

What is a bridegroom?

A person who loves and marries his wife.

What's it all about?

Jesus is the Bridegroom to the Church—all believers everywhere! He loved us so much that He died on the cross to save us. Now He wants those who follow Him to be one with Him, like a wife is with a husband.

What's an important verse about a bridegroom?

Scriptures say, "A man leaves his father and mother and is joined to his wife, and the two are united into one." This is a great mystery, but it is an illustration of the way Christ and the church are one. EPHESIANS 5:31–32 NLT

What does that mean to me?

Spend time with Jesus. The more you do, the better you'll know and love Him.

Caiaphas, the High Priest

Who is Caiaphas, the High Priest?

He was the top leader of the Jews the year Jesus was crucified.

What's it all about?

After His arrest, Jesus was taken to Caiaphas and put on trial. But Caiaphas had already decided that Jesus should be killed— which, it turns out, was part of God's plan.

What's an important verse about Caiaphas, the High Priest?

Caiaphas was the one who had told the other Jewish leaders, "It's better that one man should die for the people."
JOHN 18:14 NLT

What does that mean to me?

Leave everything in God's hands—the good and the bad—because He can use anything, anyone, and any situation to make His plans come true!

Commission to the Disciples

What is the commission to the disciples?

The job Jesus gave His disciples to do.

What's it all about?

After Jesus died and rose again, He gave His followers an order: to go all over the world and spread the word about Him.

What's an important verse about the commission to the disciples?

Jesus came to them. He said. . ."Go and make disciples of all nations. Baptize them in the name of the Father and of the Son and of the Holy Spirit. Teach them to obey everything I have commanded you. And you can be sure that I am always with you, to the very end."
MATTHEW 28:18–20

What does that mean to me?

All believers—then and now, you and me—are to spread the word about Jesus and teach people to love God and each other. He has promised to never, ever leave us as we carry out His mission!

Controls Nature

Who controls nature?

Jesus. He can stop the wind and calm the waves.

What's it all about?

Jesus and His disciples decided to cross a lake in a boat. While they were on the water, a big storm came up. The waves were very high, and the boat began filling with water. Jesus was asleep at the back of the boat. His followers got scared, began shouting, and woke Him up.

What's an important verse about controlling nature?

When Jesus woke up, he rebuked the wind and said to the waves, "Silence! Be still!" Suddenly the wind stopped, and there was a great calm. Then he asked them, "Why are you afraid? Do you still have no faith?"
MARK 4:39–40 NLT

What does that mean to me?

When storms come into your life, trust in Jesus. He's already in your boat. So don't be scared. He's in control. Have faith that He will make everything turn out all right.

Cornerstone

What is a cornerstone?

A cornerstone is a big solid rock. It is on that rock, the foundation, that people build. If this rock is removed, the whole building might crash down!

What's it all about?

Jesus is our cornerstone. He's the solid rock, the sure foundation, on which the Christian Church was built and on which we stand.

What's an important verse about a cornerstone?

You belong in God's family. This family is built on the teachings of the missionaries and the early preachers. Jesus Christ Himself is the cornerstone, which is the most important part of the building. Christ keeps this building together and it is growing into a holy building for the Lord. You are also being put together as a part of this building because God lives in you by His Spirit.
EPHESIANS 2:19–22 NLV

With Jesus as your cornerstone, you can stand up against anything—because God lives in you and you are part of His family!

Creator

Who is the Creator?

Jesus is! That's why He is so powerful!

What's it all about?

Jesus not only made everything we see; He made everything we *don't* see! And not only is He our awesome Creator, but He's our Sustainer, too. That means He keeps everything going. He made each of us and keeps us all breathing. He keeps the clouds up in the sky and the planets in the heavens.

What's an important verse about the Creator?

Christ made everything in the heavens and on the earth. He made everything that is seen and things that are not seen. He made all the powers of heaven. Everything was made by Him and for Him. Christ was before all things. All things are held together by Him.
COLOSSIANS 1:16–17 NLV

What does that mean to me?

Because Jesus is the Creator, He can help *you* with your own creations. Tap into His power. He'll make your ideas even better!

Cross

What is a cross?

A long piece of wood that has a shorter piece across it, close to the top.

What's it all about?

The Roman government punished people by nailing them to a wooden cross. The long end of the cross would be stuck in the ground, and people would hang there until they died.

What's an important verse about a cross?

We know that our old life, our old sinful self, was nailed to the cross with Christ. And so the power of sin that held us was destroyed. Sin is no longer our boss.
ROMANS 6:6 NLV

What does that mean to me?

If you believe in Jesus, you are free from sin's power! Instead, you are filled with God's power. *He's* the one who brought Jesus back to life.

Crucifixion

What is the crucifixion?

When Jesus was nailed to the cross to pay for our sins (wrongdoings).

What's it all about?

Jesus hadn't done anything wrong, but the religious leaders didn't like Him. So they got the Roman governor to crucify Jesus on the cross. It was all part of God's plan to bring us back to Him.

What's an important verse about the Crucifixion?

I have been crucified with Christ. I don't live any longer, but Christ lives in me. . . . He loved me and gave himself for me. GALATIANS 2:20

What does that mean to me?

God took the part of you that has trouble following rules and put it on the cross with Jesus Christ. When Jesus was buried, your sins were buried, too   forever!

Denial of Peter

What is the denial of Peter?

Jesus knew a follower named Peter would one day tell people he didn't know Jesus.

What's it all about?

When Jesus was arrested, Peter got scared. Three times he denied knowing Him!

What's an important verse about the denial of Peter?

Peter remembered what Jesus had said. "The rooster will crow," Jesus had told him. "Before it does, you will say three times that you don't know me." Peter went outside. He broke down and cried. MATTHEW 26:75

What does that mean to me?

Sooner or later, you may be sorry for the things you have done. When that happens, remember that Jesus, who knows all, has already forgiven you. And can still use you!

Devil

What is the devil?

A very bad (evil) spiritual being.

What's it all about?

Jesus called the devil the father of lies. He was the serpent in the Garden of Eden who talked Eve into disobeying God. And he has been tricking people ever since!

What's an important verse about the devil?

Dear children, don't let anyone lead you astray. . . . The person who does what is sinful belongs to the devil. That's because the devil has been sinning from the beginning. But the Son of God came to destroy the devil's work. 1 JOHN 3:7–8

What does that mean to me?

If you obey God and follow Jesus, the devil will lose his influence over you!

Disciples

What are disciples?

People who follow the teachings of Jesus.

What's it all about?

Jesus had 12 main disciples: Simon Peter and his brother Andrew; James, son of Zebedee, and his brother John; Philip and Bartholomew; Thomas; Matthew, the tax collector; James, son of Alphaeus; Thaddaeus; Simon, the Zealot; and Judas Iscariot.

What's an important verse about disciples?

Jesus called together the 12 disciples. He gave them power and authority to drive out all demons and to heal sicknesses. Then he sent them out to announce God's kingdom and to heal those who were sick. LUKE 9:1–2

What does that mean to me?

When you answer Jesus' calling and make Him first in your life, you, too, can be His disciple. That's some powerful stuff!

Foot Washing

What is foot washing?

When you wash your own feet or someone else's.

What's it all about?

The night before His arrest, Jesus was at dinner with His 12 disciples. Before eating, Jesus wrapped a towel around Himself, poured water into a bowl, and washed and dried all His disciples' feet.

What's an important verse about foot washing?

"Since I, your Lord and Teacher, have washed your feet, you ought to wash each other's feet. I have given you an example to follow. Do as I have done to you. I tell you the truth, slaves are not greater than their master."
JOHN 13:14–16 NLT

What does that mean to me?

True happiness comes from doing something for someone else. Who can you "do for" today?

Gabriel

Who is Gabriel?

An angel or messenger of God.

What's it all about?

In the Old Testament, Gabriel talked with Daniel. In the New Testament, God sent Gabriel to tell Zacharias he would have a son. Then God sent Gabriel with an important message for Mary.

What's an important verse about Gabriel?

Gabriel appeared to her and said, "Greetings, favored woman! The Lord is with you!" Confused and disturbed, Mary tried to think what the angel could mean. "Don't be afraid, Mary," the angel told her, "for you have found favor with God! You will conceive and give birth to a son, and you will name him Jesus." LUKE 1:28–31 NLT

What does that mean to me?

Puzzled? Don't worry. When God sends you a message, He'll make sure it's clear!

Galilee

What is Galilee?

A region in northern Israel.

What's it all about?

Jesus spent His childhood in Nazareth, a town in Galilee. Eleven of Jesus' 12 disciples (all but Judas Iscariot) and most of the women who followed Jesus came from Galilee. At a wedding in Cana, a town in Galilee, they ran out of wine. So Jesus turned water into wine.

What's an important verse about Galilee?

What Jesus did here in Cana in Galilee was the first of his signs. Jesus showed his glory by doing this sign. And his disciples believed in him. JOHN 2:11

What does that mean to me?

Jesus is so powerful that He can work miracles whenever and wherever you are. That's a faith booster!

Gethsemane

Where is Gethsemane?

This olive grove is a little way up the Mount of Olives in Jerusalem, Israel.

What's it all about?

Jesus took all but one of His disciples with Him to Gethsemane. He kept three of them even closer. In Gethsemane, Jesus prayed so hard that He sweat drops of blood. Later a mob, led by Judas Iscariot, came to arrest Him.

What's an important verse about Gethsemane?

Jesus went with them to the olive grove called Gethsemane, and he said, "Sit here while I go over there to pray." He took Peter and Zebedee's two sons, James and John, and he became anguished and distressed. . . . He went on a little farther and bowed with his face to the ground, praying. MATTHEW 26:36–37, 39 NLT

What does that mean to me?

Get closer to Jesus when you are upset or hurt. He can help you because He knows just what you are going through.

Golden Rule

What is the Golden Rule?

That we should only interact with others in ways that we would like others to act toward us.

What's it all about?

Jesus told us not only how to follow God, but also how to live with other people. We are to treat them as we would have them treat us. If everyone would do that, peace, love, and understanding would rule!

What's an important verse about the Golden Rule?

"Do for other people whatever you would like to have them do for you. This is what the Jewish Law and the early preachers said." MATTHEW 7:12 NLV

What does that mean to me?

Be good to other people—no matter how they treat you. That Golden Rule rules!

Golgotha

Where is Golgotha?

In Jesus' day, Golgotha was just outside of Jerusalem. Today, Golgotha is inside Jerusalem's walls.

What's it all about?

The Hebrew word *Golgotha* and the Latin word *Calvary* both mean "the skull." It's where Romans crucified criminals.

What's an important verse about Golgotha?

They brought Jesus to a place called Golgotha (which means "Place of the Skull"). They offered him wine drugged with myrrh, but he refused it. Then the soldiers nailed him to the cross. MARK 15:22–24 NLT

What does that mean to me?

After suffering at Golgotha, Jesus died—but then He came back to life, and He still lives today! So no matter how bad things look, don't worry or be scared. God will make good out of it!

Good Shepherd

Who is the Good Shepherd?

Jesus Christ is!

What's it all about?

Jesus is our shepherd—and we are the sheep He takes care of. He talks to our hearts so that we will know His voice and be sure to follow Him. Jesus will always protect us and watch over us. He will never leave us, and He will always give us what we need.

What's an important verse about the Good Shepherd?

"I am the Good Shepherd. The Good Shepherd gives His life for the sheep. . . . I know My sheep and My sheep know Me." JOHN 10:11, 14 NLV

What does that mean to me?

Jesus laid down His life so you could live forever. So stick close to Him. His mission is to take good care of you. Your mission? Get to know Him better by reading your Bible. Learn all you can about Him. He already knows everything about you.

Gospels–Matthew, Mark, Luke, John

What are the Gospels?

The books in the Bible that tell the life, death, and resurrection stories of Jesus.

What's it all about?

Matthew, Mark, Luke, and John each wrote a story all about Jesus and His life. These stories, or *gospels*, are the first four books of the New Testament in the Bible. Matthew wrote his story for Jews. Mark wrote for Romans. Luke wrote for non-Jews. And John wrote for all believers. The word *gospel* means "good news." Because that's what Jesus is!

What's an important verse about the Gospels?

I. . .decided to write down an orderly report of exactly what happened. I am doing this for you, most excellent Theophilus. I want you to know that the things you have been taught are true. LUKE 1:3–4

The gospel stories are exact accounts of Jesus' life. So read and believe them. They are packed full of good news for you and me!

Greatest Commandments

What are the greatest commandments?

The two most important rules Jesus wants us to follow.

What's it all about?

God gave Moses lots of laws His people were to obey. When Jesus came along, He said that His law of love would take care of all other laws.

What's an important verse about the greatest commandments?

Jesus replied, " 'You must love the LORD your God with all your heart, all your soul, and all your mind.' This is the first and greatest commandment. A second is equally important: 'Love your neighbor as yourself.' "
MATTHEW 22:37–39 NLT

What does that mean to me?

If you truly love God, yourself, and others with all that you are, you will make God, yourself, and the rest of the world happy.

Heaven

What is heaven?

A place beyond the clouds.

What's it all about?

Heaven is where God and Jesus are now. It's also where the souls and spirits of Christians go after their bodies die.

What's an important verse about heaven?

"Love your enemies! Do good to them. Lend to them without expecting to be repaid. Then your reward from heaven will be very great, and you will truly be acting as children of the Most High." LUKE 6:35 NLT

What does that mean to me?

The more you act like God here on earth, the more you will be rewarded for it in heaven—and the more you'll make your world like a little piece of heaven on earth!

Herod the Great

Who is Herod the Great?

A king of Judea who was part Jewish and part Roman.

What's it all about?

When Herod heard the "king of the Jews" (Jesus) had been born, Herod got jealous. In his eyes, there was no room for another king. So he sent soldiers to kill baby Jesus. But an angel warned Jesus' foster father, Joseph, in a dream. They escaped!

What's an important verse about Herod the Great?

After Herod died, Joseph had a dream. . . . The angel said, "Get up! Take the child and his mother. Go to the land of Israel. The people who were trying to kill the child are dead." MATTHEW 2:19–20

What does that mean to me?

Keep your ears open to God's messengers. They'll keep you safe!

Hidden Manna

What is hidden manna?

Manna is the stuff God rained down from heaven to feed the Israelites in the wilderness after they fled Egypt. Jesus is the "hidden manna."

What's it all about?

God gives us everything we need to eat, live, love, smile, and breathe. And the best thing He has blessed us with is Jesus. He is our "top-secret provision"—all we ever really need comes from and is found in Him.

What's an important verse about hidden manna?

"Anyone with ears to hear must listen to the Spirit and understand what he is saying to the churches. To everyone who is victorious I will give some of the manna that has been hidden away in heaven." REVELATION 2:17 NLT

What does that mean to me?

You can depend on Jesus to supply *everything* you need!

Holy Spirit

Who is the Holy Spirit?

God's spiritual presence living within Jesus' followers, sent to comfort, inspire, and help.

What's it all about?

When Jesus went back to heaven, He sent believers the Holy Spirit to guide them, teach them, and be their friend.

What's an important verse about the Holy Spirit?

All the believers gathered in one place. Suddenly a sound came from heaven. It was like a strong wind blowing. It filled the whole house where they were sitting. . . . All of them were filled with the Holy Spirit. Acts 2:1–2, 4

What does that mean to me?

When you became a believer, the Holy Spirit came to live inside you. So you have a very close friend. Ask Him to teach and guide you!

I Am

Who is the I Am?

God *and* Jesus.

What's it all about?

When Moses asked God what His name was, He said He was the "I Am." Later, Jesus said that He, too, was the I Am. That means God and Jesus always have been, always are, and always will be. Jesus also said He is the Bread of Life; Light of the world; Door; Good Shepherd; Resurrection and Life; the Way, the Truth, and the Life; and true Vine!

What's an important verse about the I Am?

"How can you say you have seen Abraham?" Jesus answered, "I tell you the truth, before Abraham was even born, I am!" JOHN 8:57–58 NLT

What does that mean to me?

Jesus was, is, and always will be whatever you need, wherever and whenever you need Him!

James, Son of Zebedee

Who is James, son of Zebedee?

One of Jesus' main disciples and a brother of John.

What's it all about?

James was a fisherman working with his brother John, his father Zebedee, and his friend Simon Peter. As soon as Jesus called James, he left his boat and father and went with Jesus. James, John, and Peter were very close to Jesus.

What's an important verse about James, son of Zebedee?

King Herod arrested some people who belonged to the church. He planned to make them suffer greatly. He had James killed with a sword. James was John's brother.
ACTS 12:1–2

What does that mean to me?

James loved Jesus so much that he was willing to die for Him. Does Jesus mean that much to you?

Jerusalem

Where is Jerusalem?

Also called the City of David and Zion, Jerusalem is in Israel.

What's it all about?

Jerusalem is where the temple was built. When Jesus was born, His parents took Him to the Jerusalem Temple to dedicate Him to God. Later, outside of Jerusalem's walls, Jesus was killed.

What's an important verse about Jerusalem?

Jesus began to explain to his disciples what would happen to him. He told them he must go to Jerusalem. There he. . . must be killed and on the third day rise to life again.
MATTHEW 16:21

What does that mean to me?

Jesus knows everything that has happened, is happening, and will happen—even in your life! So don't worry. He's got everything figured out, and it's all good.

John the Baptist

Who is John the Baptist?

The cousin of Jesus.

What's it all about?

An angel told Zachariah that he would have a son in his old age. Nine months later, his son, John the Baptist, was born. John lived in the wilderness and ate honey and locusts. Later, he baptized Jesus in the Jordan River.

What's an important verse about John the Baptist?

"You yourselves are witnesses that I said, 'I am not the Messiah. I was sent ahead of him'. . . . He must become more important. I must become less important."
JOHN 3:28, 30

What does that mean to me?

You are very important to Jesus. Are you willing to make Him the *most* important thing in your life?

John, Son of Zebedee

Who is John, son of Zebedee?

One of Jesus' main disciples and the brother of James.

What's it all about?

John fished with James, Zebedee, and Simon Peter. When Jesus called, John dropped the net he was mending and followed Jesus! This disciple wrote the Bible books of John and Revelation.

What's an important verse about John, son of Zebedee?

When Jesus saw his mother standing there beside the disciple he loved, he said to her, "Dear woman, here is your son." And he said to this disciple, "Here is your mother." And from then on this disciple took her into his home. JOHN 19:26–27 NLT

What does that mean to me?

Jesus trusted John with His mother. Is Jesus trusting you with someone or something?

Joseph, Foster Father of Jesus

Who is Joseph, foster father of Jesus?

A good man, carpenter, descendant of David, and husband to Mary.

What's it all about?

Joseph planned to marry Mary. But he changed his mind when he found out she was pregnant—until God's angel came to him in a dream.

What's an important verse about Joseph, foster father of Jesus?

The angel said, "Joseph, son of David, don't be afraid to take Mary home as your wife. The baby inside her is from the Holy Spirit. She is going to have a son. You must give him the name Jesus." MATTHEW 1:20–21

What does that mean to me?

Be like Joseph: keep your ears open to hear God's good plan for your life—and follow it!

Joseph of Arimathea

Who is Joseph of Arimathea?

A rich man from Arimathea.

What's it all about?

Joseph, a leader in the Jewish Council, didn't agree with the council's decision to kill Jesus. That's because Joseph was a follower of Jesus in secret. He didn't want others to know because he was afraid. Later, Joseph buried Jesus in his own tomb.

What's an important verse about Joseph of Arimathea?

Joseph went boldly to Pilate and asked for Jesus' body. . . . He took down the body and wrapped it in the linen. He put it in a tomb cut out of rock. Then he rolled a stone against the entrance. MARK 15:43, 46

What does that mean to me?

God will give you courage—just when you need it!

Judas Iscariot

Who is Judas Iscariot?

One of Jesus' main disciples *and* the one who betrayed Him.

What's it all about?

Judas didn't like some of the ways Jesus did things. So, for 30 pieces of silver, he handed Jesus over to His enemies, who then killed Him. Later, Judas hung himself.

What's an important verse about Judas Iscariot?

Judas was sorry he had handed Jesus over when he saw that Jesus was going to be killed. He took back the thirty pieces of silver and gave it to the head religious leaders and the other leaders. He said, "I have sinned because I handed over a Man Who has done no wrong." And they said, "What is that to us? That is your own doing."
MATTHEW 27:3–4 NLV

What does that mean to me?

Stay on the right and faithful path by loving God and Jesus much more than money.

Kingdom of Heaven (or God)

What is the kingdom of heaven (or God)?

The peace believers feel inside their spirits and hearts. It's also where believers will live after Jesus comes back.

What's it all about?

When we totally count on God to take care of everything in our lives, we are living in the kingdom of heaven!

What's an important verse about the kingdom of heaven (or God)?

Jesus said, "What I'm about to tell you is true. You need to change and become like little children. If you don't, you will never enter the kingdom of heaven."
MATTHEW 18:3

What does that mean to me?

No matter how things look, put *all* your trust in God. You'll find yourself in His royal palace—where He alone is King!

Lamb of God

Who is the Lamb of God?

Jesus is!

What's it all about?

In Old Testament days, God's people would kill (sacrifice) a perfect lamb. The blood of that lamb cleansed people of their sins so that they could get close to God. When Jesus died on the cross, He became *our* perfect Lamb!

What's an important verse about the Lamb of God?

The next day John the Baptist saw Jesus coming to him. He said, "See! The Lamb of God Who takes away the sin of the world!" JOHN 1:29 NLV

What does that mean to me?

Jesus shed His blood to save you from your sins. Because of Him, you can snuggle up close to God! Thank Jesus for His sacrifice today.

Last Supper

What is the Last Supper?

The last meal Jesus ate with His followers before He was killed.

What's it all about?

Hours before His arrest, Jesus and His 12 main disciples had a Passover meal in Jerusalem where Jesus washed his followers' feet. Then He told them to break bread and drink wine in memory of that night and God's new promise—that all who believe in Jesus will be saved.

What's an important verse about the Last Supper?

Jesus took bread. He gave thanks and broke it. He handed it to them [His followers] and said, "This is my body. It is given for you". . . . In the same way, after the supper he took the cup. He said, "This cup is the new covenant in my blood. It is poured out for you." LUKE 22:19–20

What does that mean to me?

Remember Jesus always. Know that He is all you need to be saved!

Lazarus

Who is Lazarus?

A brother of Mary and Martha of Bethany.

What's it all about?

Jesus loved His friend Lazarus so much that He cried when Lazarus died. Then Jesus brought His friend back to life!

What's an important verse about Lazarus?

Jesus loved Martha and her sister and Lazarus. But when He heard that Lazarus was sick, He stayed where He was two more days. . . . Then Jesus said to [His followers], "Lazarus is dead. Because of you I am glad I was not there so that you may believe. Come, let us go to him."
JOHN 11:5–6, 14–15 NLV

What does that mean to me?

Never give up hope. Jesus *will* come to help you! In His own time and all to God's glory!

Light of the World

Who is the Light of the world?

Jesus is!

What's it all about?

Jesus is not only our Savior, but He is also light! When He shines His light, we can see more clearly what is right and wrong.

What's an important verse about the Light of the world?

Jesus spoke to the people again. He said, "I am the light of the world. Anyone who follows me will never walk in darkness. They will have that light. They will have life." JOHN 8:12

What does that mean to me?

Your path is clear and your steps sure when you walk in the Light! So follow Jesus closely. He'll keep the darkness away—and help your own light to shine.

Lion of the Tribe of Judah

Who is the Lion of the tribe of Judah?

Jesus is!

What's it all about?

The name *Judah* means "to praise." Jesus, from the Jewish tribe of Judah, burst out of the grave like a lion, and all His enemies scattered! Nothing can keep Him down or hold Him back. He wins every battle.

What's an important verse about the Lion of the tribe of Judah?

"Stop weeping! Look, the Lion of the tribe of Judah, the heir to David's throne, has won the victory. He is worthy to open the scroll and its seven seals."
REVELATION 5:5 NLT

What does that mean to me?

If you have a problem, praise Jesus—your foes will flee and your load will lighten!

Living Water

What is living water?

The Spirit that enters believers in Jesus.

What's it all about?

When you let Jesus into your heart, He sends the Holy Spirit to live inside you. That Spirit is like living water. It cools down and peps up all who are thirsty for God and for doing right.

What's an important verse about living water?

Jesus stood up and spoke in a loud voice. He said, "Let anyone who is thirsty come to me and drink. Does anyone believe in me? Then, just as Scripture says, rivers of living water will flow from inside them." John 7:37–38

What does that mean to me?

Drink in Jesus and watch your doubts and fears get flushed out!

Loaves and Fishes

What are the loaves and fishes?

The miracle of the loaves and fishes is the only one that appears in all four Gospels—Matthew, Mark, Luke, and John.

What's it all about?

Five thousand hungry men, along with women and children, came to hear Jesus. But only one small boy had food—five loaves of bread and two fishes. The disciples didn't know what to do. But Jesus did! After He thanked God for the food, there was enough for all the people—plus some left over!

What's an important verse about the loaves and fishes?

Jesus. . .said to Philip, "Where can we buy bread to feed these people?" He said this to see what Philip would say. Jesus knew what He would do. Philip said to Him, "The money we have is not enough to buy bread to give each one a little." JOHN 6:5–7 NLV

What does that mean to me?

Got a problem? Go to Jesus. He already knows the answer!

Lord of Peace

Who is the Lord of peace?

Jesus is!

What's it all about?

While Jesus was here on earth, He was blamed for something He didn't do. He was beaten and laughed at. He was whipped and then hung from a cross until He died. Through all this, He kept the peace of God.

What's an important verse about the Lord of peace?

Now may the Lord of peace himself give you his peace at all times and in every situation. The Lord be with you all. 2 THESSALONIANS 3:16 NLT

What does that mean to me?

Jesus knows everything you are going through—because He went through it all! He *Himself* will give you peace. He Himself walks with you—at all times and in every situation.

Manna from Heaven

What is manna from heaven?

Jesus—He is all we need!

What's it all about?

When the wandering Israelites were hungry in the wilderness, God rained down food from heaven. People had never seen it before, so they called it *manna*, which means, "What is it?"

What's an important verse about manna from heaven?

"Your ancestors ate manna in the wilderness, but they all died. Anyone who eats the bread from heaven, however, will never die. I am the living bread that came down from heaven." JOHN 6:49–51 NLT

What does that mean to me?

If you are hungry, sad, angry, sorry, sick, in need, or feeling unloved, go to Jesus. He'll give you the one thing you need as you travel through life: nourishment from Him—forever and ever.

Martha

Who is Martha?

The sister of Mary and Lazarus of Bethany.

What's it all about?

Jesus made a visit to Martha and Mary's house. Martha was busy getting dinner ready. But Mary was doing nothing except sitting at Jesus' feet and listening to what He said. So Martha asked Jesus to make Mary help her.

What's an important verse about Martha?

"Martha, Martha," the Lord answered. "You are worried and upset about many things. . . . Only one thing is needed. Mary has chosen what is better. And it will not be taken away from her." LUKE 10:41–42

What does that mean to me?

Always make time to sit with Jesus. Just being with and listening to Him are the most important things you can do.

Mary of Bethany

Who is Mary of Bethany?

The sister of Martha and Lazarus.

What's it all about?

Mary loved listening to Jesus. After all, He was so wise and wonderful—He'd even saved her brother's life!

What's an important verse about Mary of Bethany?

Jesus came to Bethany, where Lazarus lived. Lazarus was the one Jesus had raised from the dead. . . . Then Mary took about a pint of pure nard. It was an expensive perfume. She poured it on Jesus' feet and wiped them with her hair. The house was filled with the sweet smell of the perfume. JOHN 12:1, 3

What does that mean to me?

Nothing is too good for Jesus. What special thing can *you* do for Him today?

Mary, the Mother of Jesus

Who is Mary, the mother of Jesus?

She is the virgin who gave birth to Jesus, the Son of God, and who married Joseph the carpenter.

What's it all about?

Mary was engaged to Joseph. The angel Gabriel told her she would get pregnant and become the mother of Jesus. Gabriel also told Mary that her cousin Elizabeth was pregnant—and that with God, anything is possible!

What's an important verse about Mary, the mother of Jesus?

Mary said to the angel, "How will this happen? I have never had a man." The angel said to her, "The Holy Spirit will come on you. . . . For God can do all things." Then Mary said, "I am willing to be used of the Lord. Let it happen to me as you have said." Then the angel went away from her. LUKE 1:34–35, 37–38 NLV

What does that mean to me?

Believe God can do the impossible—through you. And He will!

Mary Magdalene

Who is Mary Magdalene?

A follower of Jesus and the first to see Him resurrected.

What's it all about?

After Jesus had chased seven demons out of Mary Magdalene, she followed Him everywhere. She watched Jesus being crucified and buried. But there was hope!

What's an important verse about Mary Magdalene?

Jesus said to her, "Mary! . . . Go to My brothers. Tell them that I will go up to My Father and your Father, and to My God and your God!" Mary Magdalene went and told the followers that she had seen the Lord.
JOHN 20:16–18 NLV

What does that mean to me?

Mary became a messenger to the messengers of the Good News. With whom can you share the hope of Jesus?

Matthew

Who is Matthew?

First he was a tax collector, then he became one of Jesus' main disciples. He wrote the Bible book of Matthew.

What's it all about?

In Jesus' day, tax collectors usually cheated people. And that's what Matthew did. Even so, Jesus told Matthew to follow Him. Then He had dinner with other sinners at Matthew's house.

What's an important verse about Matthew?

But when the Pharisees saw this, they asked his disciples, "Why does your teacher eat with such scum?" When Jesus heard this, he said. . . . "I have come to call not those who think they are righteous, but those who know they are sinners." MATTHEW 9:11–13 NLT

What does that mean to me?

For Jesus, there is no lost cause when it comes to people. Who can you bring out the best in today?

Messiah

What is a messiah?

The word *messiah* means "the anointed one." In Greek, the word means "Christ." It's a term for a person who is set apart to serve God and is anointed with oil.

What's it all about?

In the Old Testament, prophets told the Jews that someone in David's family would forever rule God's people. So the Jews began looking for this forever messiah. Thousands of years later, the Messiah was born and called Jesus Christ.

What's an important verse about a messiah?

The woman said, "I know that Messiah is coming." Messiah means Christ. "When he comes, he will explain everything to us." Then Jesus said, "The one you're talking about is the one speaking to you. I am he."
JOHN 4:25–26

What does that mean to me?

Are you ever confused? That's okay. Just go to Jesus. He's the King of all kings. He knows the answers to all your questions. He will show Himself to you and explain everything.

Miracle Worker

Who is the Miracle Worker?

Jesus is, was, and always will be!

What's it all about?

Jesus, the Son of God, had the power to heal people, chase demons, calm the wind, smooth out the sea, turn water into wine, raise the dead, and multiply loaves and fishes. Later, His followers did miracles, too—in Jesus' name!

What's an important verse about the Miracle Worker?

Jesus asked them, "Do you believe I can make you see?" "Yes, Lord," they told him, "we do." Then he touched their eyes and said, "Because of your faith, it will happen." Then their eyes were opened, and they could see!
MATTHEW 9:28–30 NLT

What does that mean to me?

If you have faith, Jesus can work a miracle in your life! Only believe!

Money Changers

Who are money changers?

Men who gave people Roman coins for Hebrew ones so that worshippers could buy an animal to sacrifice to God in the temple.

What's it all about?

Jesus believed that people should only be worshipping, praying, preaching, and learning about God in the temple—for it was *His* house, not a store where things could be bought and sold.

What's an important verse about money changers?

So Jesus. . .scattered the coins of the people exchanging money. And he turned over their tables. He told those who were selling doves, "Get these out of here! Stop turning my Father's house into a market!"
JOHN 2:15–16

What does that mean to me?

When in church, focus on God—not money.

Nativity

The birth of Jesus in Bethlehem. It's what we celebrate at Christmastime.

What's it all about?

Jesus, the one who would save the world, came in the form of a small, helpless baby born in a barn. Yet His coming was announced by an angel and a star led wise men to Him. They came and brought Him gifts. Shepherds also came to see the Lord of all.

What's an important verse about the Nativity?

While Joseph and Mary were there, the time came for the child to be born. She gave birth to her first baby. It was a boy. She wrapped him in large strips of cloth. Then she placed him in a manger. That's because there was no guest room where they could stay. LUKE 2:6–7

What does that mean to me?

Have you made room for Jesus in your heart? If not, why not make Him the star of your life today?

Nazareth

Where is Nazareth?

In Galilee.

What's it all about?

Nazareth is Jesus' hometown. That's why He was called Jesus of Nazareth.

What's an important verse about Nazareth?

Jesus left there and went to his hometown of Nazareth. His disciples went with him. . . . Jesus laid his hands on a few sick people and healed them. But he could not do any other miracles there. He was amazed because they had no faith. MARK 6:1, 5–6

What does that mean to me?

By not believing in Jesus, the people of Nazareth shut off His miracle-working power. Are you blocking Jesus' power in your life? Open up all of yourself to Him today and watch what He can do!

Nicodemus

Who is Nicodemus?

A Jewish ruler or Pharisee.

What's it all about?

Nicodemus was curious about Jesus, so he went to visit Him one night. Later, Nicodemus spoke up for Jesus when his fellow leaders wanted to arrest the Lord.

What's an important verse about Nicodemus?

Nicodemus went with Joseph. He was the man who had earlier visited Jesus at night. Nicodemus brought some mixed spices that weighed about 75 pounds. The two men took Jesus' body. They wrapped it in strips of linen cloth, along with the spices. JOHN 19:39–40

What does that mean to me?

The more you hang out with Jesus, the more you get to know Him and love Him. The more you know Him, the more you'll want to serve Him. Spend time with Jesus today. You'll be glad you did!

153 Fishes

What are the 153 fishes?

The number of fish Jesus' fishermen-followers caught.

What's it all about?

The followers of Jesus didn't know what to do after Jesus rose from the dead, so they went back to their jobs as fishermen. That night they didn't catch anything. The next morning, a stranger stood on the lakeshore. He told them where to cast their fishing net. They obeyed and caught 153 fish! *Then* they realized the stranger was Jesus.

What's an important verse about the 153 fishes?

Simon Peter went out and pulled the net to land. There were 153 big fish. The net was not broken even with so many. Jesus said to them, "Come and eat." Not one of the followers would ask, "Who are You?" They knew it was the Lord. JOHN 21:11–12 NLV

What does that mean to me?

With Jesus nearby, you'll have success. Just do what He says!

Parables

What are parables?

Stories using ordinary things to teach extraordinary lessons.

What's it all about?

Jesus told lots of parables so that people could understand what He was trying to teach them.

What's an important verse about parables?

Jesus always used stories and illustrations like these when speaking to the crowds. In fact, he never spoke to them without using such parables. This fulfilled what God had spoken through the prophet: "I will speak to you in parables. I will explain things hidden since the creation of the world." MATTHEW 13:34–35 NLT

What does that mean to me?

The more parables you understand, the more power you'll reveal in God's Word and the more secrets you'll know! What parable can you read—and share—today?

Paul (or Saul)

Who is Paul (or Saul)?

A Jewish leader named Saul who turned into a Christian named Paul.

What's it all about?

Saul was taking followers of Jesus to prison—or killing them! But one day God struck Saul blind and changed his heart—and life—forever.

What's an important verse about Paul (or Saul)?

Ananias. . .said, "Brother Saul, the Lord Jesus, who appeared to you on the road, has sent me so that you might regain your sight and be filled with the Holy Spirit." Instantly something like scales fell from Saul's eyes, and he regained his sight. Then he got up and was baptized. ACTS 9:17–18 NLT

What does that mean to me?

No matter what you've done, God can still use you!

Philip

Who is Philip?

A fisherman from Bethsaida and one of Jesus' main disciples.

What's it all about?

Right after he began following Jesus, Philip invited others to meet Him.

What's an important verse about Philip?

Philip went to look for Nathanael and told him, "We have found the very person Moses and the prophets wrote about! His name is Jesus, the son of Joseph from Nazareth." "Nazareth!" exclaimed Nathanael. "Can anything good come from Nazareth?" "Come and see for yourself," Philip replied. JOHN 1:45–46 NLT

What does that mean to me?

Jesus wants many to be saved before He comes to visit us again. There's no time to lose! Who can you introduce Jesus to today?

Pontius Pilate

Who is Pontius Pilate?

A Roman governor of Judea.

What's it all about?

Jewish leaders wanted Pontius Pilate to crucify Jesus. Pilate's wife had a dream about Jesus and asked her husband not to kill Him. But even though Pilate knew Jesus was innocent, Pilate caved to the crowds and religious rulers.

What's an important verse about Pontius Pilate?

The people's shouts won out. So Pilate decided to give them what they wanted. . . . Pilate handed Jesus over to them so they could carry out their plans. LUKE 23:23–25

What does that mean to me?

Jesus wants you to stand up for what you believe in—even if you go against the crowd. So when it comes to choosing, choose Jesus—and you'll be on the right side every time.

Prayer

What is prayer?

Talking with God.

What's it all about?

God wants us to talk with Him! We can do that through prayer. Even if you don't know how to pray, God knows your heart. He'll understand what you are trying to say. And don't forget to pray in Jesus' name. Why? Check out this next verse!

What's an important verse about prayer?

"My Father will give you whatever you ask in My name. Until now you have not asked for anything in My name. Ask and you will receive. Then your joy will be full." JOHN 16:23–24

What does that mean to me?

Give your worries, thanks, joys, hopes, dreams, and blessings to God in prayer. Have faith that He has heard you. Then listen to what *He* has to say in return.

Preacher

What is a preacher?

Someone who gives people a message or sermon about God and the Good News of Jesus.

What's it all about?

Jesus preached in many places. He got many of His ideas across by telling parables, simple stories that ordinary people could understand.

What's an important verse about a preacher?

Preach the word. Be ready to serve God in good times and bad. Correct people's mistakes. Warn them. Encourage them with words of hope. Be very patient as you do these things. Teach them carefully. 2 Timothy 4:2

What does that mean to me?

One of the best ways to preach is to simply be a good example to others. Begin by following the Golden Rule. Then let your words *and* life "tell" other people about the Good News of Jesus.

Prodigal Son Parable

What is the Prodigal Son Parable?

A story Jesus told about a father and two sons.

What's it all about?

The younger son asked his dad for his half of the family money. Then this son went away and spent it all. He ended up so poor that he was not even able to afford *pig's* food. So he decided to go home, tell his dad he made a mistake, and ask him for a job. The dad not only welcomed his son back home but also celebrated his return!

What's an important verse about the Prodigal Son Parable?

"While the son was still a long way off, his father saw him. He was filled with tender love for his son. He ran to him. He threw his arms around him and kissed him."
LUKE 15:20

What does that mean to me?

If you feel lost, go to God. He welcomes all who come home to Him with arms wide open.

Resurrection

What is the Resurrection?

When Jesus rose up from the grave three days after He died on the cross.

What's it all about?

After His friend Lazarus died, Jesus resurrected him—He brought Lazarus back from the dead. After Jesus died, His body was taken down from the cross and put in a tomb that was closed up by a big rock. Three days later, the stone was rolled away, and God's power raised Jesus from the dead. Many people saw Jesus alive. That is *the* Resurrection!

What's an important verse about the Resurrection?

Jesus told her, "I am the resurrection and the life. Anyone who believes in me will live, even after dying."
JOHN 11:25 NLT

What does that mean to me?

Without Jesus in our lives, our spirits are dead. Believe in Him today, and your spirit will live forever!

Road to Emmaus

What is the road to Emmaus?

The seven-mile road leading from Jerusalem to Emmaus, about a two-hour walk.

What's it all about?

Two of Jesus' followers were walking to Emmaus three days after Jesus had died. A stranger joined them. He asked why they were so sad. So they told him everything that had happened to Jesus and invited the stranger to dinner. Then something amazing happened. . . .

What's an important verse about the road to Emmaus?

The two from Emmaus told their story of how Jesus had appeared to them as they were walking along the road, and how they had recognized him as he was breaking the bread. And just as they were telling about it, Jesus himself was suddenly standing there among them. "Peace be with you," he said. LUKE 24:35–36 NLT

What does that mean to me?

Whenever and wherever Jesus shows up, peace and joy follow!

Rock

Who is the Rock?

Jesus. He protects and strengthens us.

What's it all about?

Jesus is the Rock we can build our lives on. He is our spiritual Rock. Nothing—and no one—can topple Him!

What's an important verse about the Rock?

"So then, everyone who hears my words and puts them into practice is like a wise man. He builds his house on the rock. The rain comes down. The water rises. The winds blow and beat against that house. But it does not fall. It is built on the rock." MATTHEW 7:24–25

What does that mean to me?

Don't just listen to the Word—live it! Stand on it! And you'll be rock solid!

Savior

Who is the Savior?

Jesus Christ is—He rescued us!

What's it all about?

People couldn't obey all the laws of Moses. We kept sinning, or "missing the mark," which kept us separated from God. So God sent Jesus to earth, and Jesus sacrificed (gave up) His life to save ours.

What's an important verse about the Savior?

For God saved us and called us to live a holy life. . . . He has made all of this plain to us by the appearing of Christ Jesus, our Savior. He broke the power of death and illuminated the way to life and immortality through the Good News. 2 TIMOTHY 1:9–10

What does that mean to me?

Believe in Jesus, and He will be your Savior forever and ever!

Second Coming

What is the Second Coming?

When Jesus returns for the last time.

What's it all about?

Jesus will come back again. When He does, believers—living and dead—will rise up and join Him forever and ever in heaven.

What's an important verse about the Second Coming?

Christ was offered up once. He took away the sins of many people. He will also come a second time. At that time he will not suffer for sin. Instead, he will come to bring salvation to those who are waiting for him.
Hebrews 9:28

What does that mean to me?

You can always trust Jesus. He's someone worth waiting for—whether in heaven or on earth.

Sermon on the Mount

What is the Sermon on the Mount?

A message Jesus gave while standing on a hill. You can read His full sermon in Matthew 5–7.

What's it all about?

The Sermon on the Mount tells people how they should live for God. It's not just about doing a certain thing (on the outside), but also being a certain way (on the inside). Only someone who truly believes in Jesus can live according to the Sermon on the Mount.

What's an important verse about the Sermon on the Mount?

Jesus went up on the mountainside and sat down. His disciples gathered around him, and he began to teach them. MATTHEW 5:1–2 NLT

What does that mean to me?

Do you believe in Jesus   from the inside out?

Simon of Cyrene

Who is Simon of Cyrene?

The man who helped Jesus carry His cross to Golgotha.

What's it all about?

Jesus had been beaten, whipped, and laughed at. Then He was made to carry His heavy wooden cross to the place where He would be crucified. At some point, Jesus needed help.

What's an important verse about Simon of Cyrene?

A man named Simon, who was from Cyrene, happened to be coming in from the countryside. The soldiers seized him and put the cross on him and made him carry it behind Jesus. LUKE 23:26 NLT

What does that mean to me?

We must carry our own cross to follow Jesus. That means working with and for Him as His servants. Who can you help along the way?

Simon Peter

Who is Simon Peter?

A brother to Andrew, a fisherman, and one of Jesus' main disciples. His name means "rock."

What's it all about?

Peter really loved Jesus. Even though he made lots of mistakes—like sinking in the sea for lack of faith and later denying he even *knew* Jesus—Jesus used Peter to build up the Church.

What's an important verse about Simon Peter?

Those who believed what Peter said were baptized and added to the church that day—about 3,000 in all.
ACTS 2:41 NLT

What does that mean to me?

If you make a mistake, don't fret. Go to Jesus. Ask for His help in making things right, and He'll use you to lead others to Him.

Son of David

Who is the Son of David?

Jesus—our prophet, priest, and king! Through His mother, Mary, Jesus is an heir of David by blood. Through His foster father, Joseph, Jesus is in line for King David's throne!

What's it all about?

Many years ago, God promised King David's throne and kingdom would last forever. So Jews knew that the one who would save them (the Messiah) would be from David's family.

What's an important verse about the Son of David?

This is the written story of the family line of Jesus the Messiah. He is the son of David. MATTHEW 1:1

What does that mean to me?

Don't worry about anything. God is in control and keeps His promises and plans. Just obey King Jesus, and all will be well!

Son of God

Who is the Son of God?

Jesus—our friend and king!

What's it all about?

Jesus was conceived in Mary by the Holy Spirit. That makes Him God's Son. And Jesus is just like His Father God!

What's an important verse about the Son of God?

As soon as Jesus was baptized. . .heaven was opened. Jesus saw the Spirit of God coming down on him like a dove. A voice from heaven said, "This is my Son, and I love him. I am very pleased with him." MATTHEW 3:16–17

What does that mean to me?

When you believe in Jesus, you become one of God's children—which makes you Jesus' brother or sister! Welcome to an amazing family!

Son of Man

Who is the Son of Man?

Jesus—our brother and lord!

What's it all about?

Jesus told His followers He was the Son of Man, or Messiah, the prophet Daniel saw many years ago. As the Son of Man, Jesus was one of us—even though He was also God. Being part human, Jesus felt everything we feel.

What's an important verse about the Son of Man?

Jesus replied, "Foxes have dens. Birds have nests. But the Son of Man has no place to lay his head."
LUKE 9:58

What does that mean to me?

Jesus wants a home in you. Make room for Him in your heart, and feel free to tell Him everything you feel. He understands!

Spirit of Christ

What is the Spirit of Christ?

Having the Spirit of God living in you, making you like Jesus.

What's it all about?

When you let Jesus into your heart, the Holy Spirit comes inside you. He helps guide you to where God wants you to go by molding you to be like Jesus Christ.

What's an important verse about the Spirit of Christ?

But you are not ruled by the power of sin. Instead, the Holy Spirit rules over you. This is true if the Spirit of God lives in you. Anyone who does not have the Spirit of Christ does not belong to Christ. ROMANS 8:9

What does that mean to me?

Follow in Jesus' footsteps, and you will never be lost.

Teacher

What is a teacher?

Someone who helps you to learn.

What's it all about?

Many people—both friends and enemies—called Jesus "teacher." He told lots of parables. Some listened only to try to trick Him; others just wanted to learn more about God.

What's an important verse about a teacher?

"And don't address anyone here on earth as 'Father,' for only God in heaven is your spiritual Father. And don't let anyone call you 'Teacher,' for you have only one teacher, the Messiah." MATTHEW 23:9–10

What does that mean to me?

Jesus is the greatest of your teachers. Make sure that His lessons are the main ones you learn.

Temple Dedication

What is temple dedication?

When a baby was dedicated (committed) to God in the Jerusalem Temple.

What's it all about?

Jewish law said that babies were to be presented to God in the temple when they were eight days old. So Joseph and Mary took Jesus there, along with two birds to sacrifice. Two people at the temple—Simeon and Anna—knew Jesus was someone special right away, that He had been sent by God to rescue His people.

What's an important verse about temple dedication?

Jesus' parents were amazed at what was being said about him. LUKE 2:33 NLT

What does that mean to me?

You know Jesus is special, too! Is what you are saying about Him amazing others?

Temptation

What is temptation?

When someone or something urges you to do something you shouldn't do.

What is it all about?

After His baptism, the Spirit led Jesus into the wilderness. For forty days He ate nothing and was tempted three times by the devil. The devil tried to get Jesus to:
- doubt His Father God's care,
- accept the world and worship him (the devil) alone, and
- test God's protection.

With each temptation, Jesus defeated the devil by quoting a verse from the Bible.

What is an important verse about temptation?

Jesus said to the devil, "Get behind Me, Satan! For it is written, 'You must worship the Lord your God. You must obey Him only.'" Luke 4:8 NLV

Get to know your Bible. Then you, too, can beat the devil and put him behind you!

Thomas

Who is Thomas?

One of Jesus' main disciples, who was also called the Twin.

What's it all about?

After Jesus rose from the dead, He appeared to His disciples—but Thomas wasn't there. When the others told Thomas that the Lord had appeared to them, Thomas didn't believe them. So the Lord came again eight days later. Then Thomas *did* believe!

What's an important verse about Thomas?

"Don't be faithless any longer. Believe!". . . Then Jesus told him, "You believe because you have seen me. Blessed are those who believe without seeing me."
JOHN 20:27, 29 NLT

What does that mean to me?

How wonderful that you believe in Jesus—even though you haven't seen Him! That makes you an extra-special believer to Jesus.

Tomb

What is a tomb?

A place where people were buried.

What's it all about?

Joseph of Arimathea had a tomb carved out of rock. After laying Jesus' dead body in the tomb, Joseph rolled a big stone in front of it so that no one could get in. But when women went to visit the grave three days later, the stone had been rolled away!

What's an important verse about a tomb?

The angel said, "Don't be alarmed. You are looking for Jesus of Nazareth, who was crucified. He isn't here! He is risen from the dead!" MARK 16:6 NLT

What does that mean to me?

Jesus Christ is alive—and always will be. That's something to cheer about, for nothing can hold Him down—not even death!

Transfiguration

What is the Transfiguration?

When Jesus was so transformed that His face was as bright as the sun and His clothes were as white as light.

What's it all about?

Jesus took His followers Peter, James, and John to a mountaintop. His appearance was transfigured. Just then Moses and Elijah appeared and began talking with Jesus. A cloud came down from heaven and surrounded them all.

What's an important verse about the Transfiguration?

A bright cloud covered them. A voice from the cloud said, "This is my Son, and I love him. I am very pleased with him. Listen to him!" MATTHEW 17:5

What does that mean to me?

If you listen to Jesus, you, too, will be transformed—and that'll please God!

The Trinity

What is the Trinity?

God is three persons in one: the Father, Jesus the Son, and the Holy Spirit.

What's it all about?

God's power helps us stick close to Jesus. Jesus shows us how to live. The Holy Spirit is God's pledge that we will receive all He promised.

What's an important verse about the Trinity?

God is the One Who makes our faith and your faith strong in Christ. He has set us apart for Himself. He has put His mark on us to show we belong to Him. His Spirit is in our hearts to prove this.
2 CORINTHIANS 1:21–22 NLV

What does that mean to me?

If you're a believer, God, Jesus, and the Spirit are all on your side—inside and out!

Triumphal Entry

What is the Triumphal Entry?

When Jesus rode a donkey into Jerusalem, five days before going to the cross. We know and celebrate it today as Palm Sunday.

What's it all about?

Prophets long ago had predicted Jesus' Triumphal Entry. In all four Gospels, you can read the story about how people cheered Him and threw palm branches on the road in front of Him.

What's an important verse about the Triumphal Entry?

Jesus found a young donkey and sat on it. The Holy Writings say, "Do not be afraid, people of Jerusalem. See! Your King comes sitting on a young donkey!"
JOHN 12:14–15 NLV

What does that mean to me?

Your humble Savior and King is not gone—so do not fear, but cheer! He lives forever in heaven—and in your heart!

Two Thieves

Who are the two thieves?

Criminals crucified with Jesus, one on each side.

What's it all about?

The first thief made fun of Jesus, but the second thief yelled at the first for mocking God. The second thief knew that he and the other thief were guilty of their crimes and that Jesus was not. He knew he had no hope—except for Jesus.

What's an important verse about the two thieves?

He said to Jesus, "Lord, remember me when You come into Your holy nation." Jesus said to him, "For sure, I tell you, today you will be with Me in Paradise."
LUKE 23:42–43 NLV

What does that mean to me?

Jesus suffered to bring all to Paradise who are true of heart and believe in Him. Do you believe?

Vine

Who is the Vine?

Jesus! And God is the gardener.

Jesus, the Word made flesh, is the true Vine. He has been planted in the earth. From Him, we believers, the branches, get all our support, food, and water. With Jesus holding us up and feeding us, we can bear fruit!

What's an important verse about the Vine?

"No branch can give fruit by itself. It has to get life from the vine. You are able to give fruit only when you have life from Me. I am the Vine and you are the branches. Get your life from Me. Then I will live in you and you will give much fruit. You can do nothing without Me."
JOHN 15:4–5 NLV

What does that mean to me?

If you stick close to Jesus and keep His Word in your heart, you'll be able to do what He calls you to do, *and* you'll bring glory to God!

Walks on Water

Who walks on water?

Jesus—and Peter, for a moment or two!

What's it all about?

Jesus' followers were rowing their boat. Then the wind picked up, and the waves started to grow bigger. Next thing His followers knew, they saw Jesus walking toward their boat. Peter started walking on the water but then took his eyes off Jesus.

What's an important verse about walking on water?

Peter called to him, "Lord, if it's really you, tell me to come to you, walking on the water." "Yes, come," Jesus said. So Peter went over the side of the boat and walked on the water toward Jesus. But when he saw the strong wind and the waves, he was terrified and began to sink. "Save me, Lord!" he shouted. Jesus immediately reached out and grabbed him. MATTHEW 14:28–31 NLT

What does that mean to me?

Never fear. Jesus is near. Just keep your eyes on Him. He will save you!

Way, Truth, and Life

Who is the Way, the Truth, and the Life?

Jesus is!

What's it all about?

Jesus is the Way; in Him, God and man are brought together. He is the Truth; He is right and honest. He is the Life; for our spirits only come alive through Christ in God.

What's an important verse about the Way, the Truth, and the Life?

Thomas said to Jesus, "Lord, we do not know where You are going. How can we know the way to get there?" Jesus said, "I am the Way and the Truth and the Life. No one can go to the Father except by Me."
JOHN 14:5–6 NLV

What does that mean to me?

Jesus is all you ever need, so make your *way* through *life* in *truth* with Him!

Wise Men

Who are the wise men?

Really smart men who followed a star.

What's it all about?

Wise men were looking for the King of the Jews. So King Herod told them to let him know when they found Him, because Herod wanted to kill Him.

What's an important verse about the wise men?

The Wise Men. . .saw the child with his mother Mary. They bowed down and worshiped him. Then they opened their treasures. They gave him gold, frankincense and myrrh. But God warned them in a dream not to go back to Herod. So they returned to their country on a different road. MATTHEW 2:11–12

What does that mean to me?

No one can outsmart God. Follow Him and His Word, and you'll be wise, too!

Woman Who Bled

Who is the woman who bled?

A woman who had been bleeding for 12 years.

What's it all about?

No doctors could cure her, so this woman looked for Jesus, found Him, and reached for His robe. She was *sure* He could heal her. As soon as she touched Him, she stopped bleeding!

What's an important verse about the woman who bled?

Jesus knew that power had gone from Him. . . . He said to her, "Daughter, your faith has healed you. Go in peace and be free from your sickness." MARK 5:30, 34

What does that mean to me?

When you have faith in Jesus and reach out for Him, His power will make amazing things happen. Reach out today!

The Word

Who is the Word?

Jesus is!

What's it all about?

Jesus has been around since the beginning of time. He was with God when He spoke, creating the earth and heavens. And then the Word (Jesus Christ) became human and lived on earth. He—the Word—tells us what God wants us to know.

What's an important verse about the Word?

The Word (Christ) was in the beginning. The Word was with God. The Word was God. He was with God in the beginning. . . . Christ became human flesh and lived among us. JOHN 1:1–2, 14 NLV

What does that mean to me?

Jesus always was, is, and will be here for you. That's a good word you can hold in your heart forever and ever.

Zion

What is Zion?

Another name for Jerusalem, parts of Jerusalem, its people, and the eternal city of God.

Jesus is
- the King the prophets said would come into the City of Zion, riding on a donkey,
- the Lamb who would stand on Mount Zion, and
- the Stone in Zion.

In Scripture it says, "Look! I am placing a stone in Zion. It is a chosen and very valuable stone. It is the most important stone in the building. The one who trusts in him will never be put to shame." 1 PETER 2:6

Be proud of the strength of Jesus. When you make Him the most important thing in your life, your Cornerstone, the love of God will shine through and in you—whether you are on earth or in heaven!

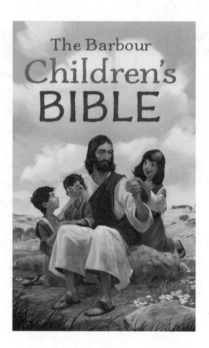